MASTERING MEDIUMSHIP

From Beginner to Professional

D1471794

ALBERT OLSON

Intuitive Revelations Publications

Acknowledgments

I would like to thank my wonderful wife whose inspiration and encouragement allowed me to not only write this book but who has also has been a partner on my personal spiritual journey.

I would also like to thank my mentor and good friend, Reverend Malcolm Gloster whose support and encouragement has allowed me to become the medium I am today.

Dedication

I would like to dedicate this book to all those mediums out there who are on this amazing journey. I hope that you will find something in these pages that will help you become the best medium that you can be. Please let me know if I can help you in any way.

Table of Contents

PREFACE

So something happened and suddenly you realize that you have been selected to receive a gift, an amazing gift that evolves over time. A gift that is different, that is hard to explain, perhaps a bit spooky, for sure exciting and sometimes scary. Some other thing happens and suddenly, you become aware that you are an intuitive or a psychic or that you have e.s.p. but you do not really know what that means. On the other side, the spirits realize that you are able to and that you are willing to communicate their messages to their loved ones on earth. Before you know it, you have become very busy, you sense spirits all around you all the time. They trust you, and they rely on you to convey their messages. Thus, a psychic/medium is born. But now what do you do? Please be patient. The path of the medium is a long and never ending one. This is a path full of thousands of baby steps that add up over time. It is a journey of spiritual discovery. In mediumship, there is no final destination, just one incredible process of evolution. A journey of a thousand miles begins with a single step. Take the first step on your journey, and turn the page.

Mastering Mediumship

Book 1 - Beginner   Albert Olson

WHY AM I ON THIS JOURNEY?

Perhaps you have a special inclination toward psychic awareness and perhaps you want to refine your abilities to a more advanced level. Like everything else in life, it is up to you to train your intuition to whatever degree you are willing to reach for. For me, it is important to share my gifts and to help people and spirits using mediumship to provide healing.

After a long journey I found some things about mediumship to be universally true. I have learned, sometimes the hard way, that every medium works differently and eventually they develop their own belief system. The only "right" way for each of us to do mediumship is to do what works best for us personally. I can pay thousands of dollars for training after which I can at best be a second rate Tony Stockwell or Mavis Pittilla or Lisa Williams but if I choose to find out what works best for me then I will always be the very best medium I can be. At first I was not sure if I was just making up my messages, but after many readings and a lot of verification from the people that I gave messages to, I came to believe that the messages I now receive are in fact from spirit. For example one of the first messages I received was for my mother-in-law Fay. At first she was a little skeptical that I had suddenly become a medium and so I was trying very hard to show her that I was legitimate. My first attempt at doing a reading for her was not that convincing. It is hard to do a reading for someone you have known for forty years because it is hard to come up with original evidence about something that I did not already know about her. We had shared so many memories and I had heard all the family stories. To make it worse the spirit coming through was her mom, Katie, who I also knew really well. After the reading I was very frustrated because I was not able to receive convincing evidence. However that night while meditating, I was visited by Fay's friend and family priest Father Andy. He showed me a bible and a family tree and gave me a message to give to Fay. The images of the bible and the family tree meant nothing to me and so I began to worry that I was making them up and that when I told Fay about them that she would think that I was a fake. However, the next day I called her and told her about my visit from Father Andy. I told her that he showed me a black bible with an inscription in it. I held my breath, waiting for her response. I was shocked when she almost yelled in my ear, "Oh, my god that was the bible he gave me!" I was relieved and happy. Fay had just confirmed that I was not making things up, that I was in fact a medium. Then I added, "He also showed me a family tree, does that mean anything to you?" Again, she answered in a very excited voice, "Yes, there is a section at the back of the bible where you can add your family tree and Father Andy encouraged me to fill it out, so I did." I felt so validated. It was at this point in my journey that

I knew that I was not making things up. I have found over the years that the fear of making things up or the fear of being a fraud are both huge barriers that almost all mediums face at some time in their development. The only way to overcome this fear and to allow yourself to continue to develop is through an activity I call, "Just make it up!" Or "Just Pretend". I know this sounds like exactly the opposite of what we want to do but trust me this works. When I see one of my students struggling to give a reading because their logical mind is telling them that they are a fake and that they cannot do mediumship at all, I say to them, "I want you to use your imagination, take a few deep breaths and ask your logical mind to take a five minute coffee break. Then I want you to continue with your reading but this time clear your mind and then just make it up. Pretend you are a great medium and put together a story for the spirit that has come through." My students usually look at me as if I am insane. I then tell them that one of two things will happen when they make it up. Either the person receiving the message will say, "No, I do not understand that" or they will be able to take your "pretend" story as evidence for the spirit coming through. For example, Sandra is a beginning medium and she is doing a reading but is really struggling to get any evidence. I ask what the problem is and she tells me that her logical mind is telling her she is making the reading up. I then say to her exactly what I just wrote above. I instruct her to tell her logical mind to take a coffee break, then to take a few deep breaths and ask her to clear her mind. Finally I ask her to continue with the reading but this time just make up the evidence and to see what happens. She begins with, "I have a tall man here dressed in an old fashioned suit and he is wearing a clown mask with bright red hair." Now I am sure that Sandra thinks that there is no possible way that this piece of evidence will mean anything to anyone. She looks at me with a face that says, "I told you I was making it up." I say to her well, one of two things is going to happen. Either no one will be reminded of a loved one on the other side or someone is going to take this piece of evidence. If no one takes it, then Sandra was right and she was making it up but if someone does take the evidence then Sandra is connected to spirit and the idea of a well dressed clown was given to her from spirit. There is an awkward moment as we wait to see what is going to happen and then she becomes totally surprised when someone in the audience says, "Yeah, I can take that." Later on the person who received the message tells us all that her grandfather used to dress up as a red headed clown for family birthday parties. In fact what Sandra thought she had made up was the most important or "wow" piece of evidence that connected the spirit to the receiver of the message.

Usually when I am doing readings I start with an opening prayer and once I have said the prayer this is when I become open to receive messages. It is like a switch is turned on in my head. A light switch that turns on an imaginary large neon sign inside my head that says, "Open for business". Once this light goes on then I am open to receive messages. This becomes part of my boundary setting that I do with spirits. Which I will speak about more fully later on in this book. This is like a beacon of light telling spirit that now is the time to connect with me. Once this prayer is over, then I believe that anything that comes into my head is divinely inspired and comes from spirit. Even if it is a tall well-dressed gentleman wearing a clown mask with red hair.

I discovered that spirits have to train their abilities just as we have to master ours. A spirit is usually drawn to someone for whom it has an affinity. Remember that, "like attracts like," and spirits, like people, will connect with mediums they understand and who they feel will understand them. This became very apparent to me one weekend when I was working at a spirit fair. This spirit fair was held in a community hall and had many different types of mediums, psychics, healers and many other practitioners or vendors. We had each paid a flat rate to have a table which we could use as a home base to offer our services from. I was one of many psychic/mediums there that weekend. People paid a small entry free and then went around from table to table to buy things or to have readings. I was a bit nervous because this was my first spirit fair and I was not sure if anyone would want a reading from me when there were so many other more experienced mediums there.

What I found though was that I had my fair share of adult clients but what amazed me most was that almost all children who were getting readings came to me. I was also amazed at how many of my readings that weekend were messages from children in spirit. Upon reflection I think this happened because I had been a school teacher for over thirty years and as a result I have a very good rapport with children and teenagers.

I believe that anyone can become a medium. The only difference between a beginner and a more advanced medium is that the advanced medium has learned to use their gifts really well. Mediumship is like any other skill it can be learned and developed. Just like every student in my classrooms over the years have been uniquely different, each medium also has their own unique way of communicating with spirit and this can change over time and from spirit to spirit.

Think about your friends and family who have died. Many of them have likely been sending you signs quite frequently and for a long time. These signs are meant to reassure you they are okay, or to let you know they are watching over you and your family, or perhaps they could provide you with a solution to a problem. Some people see the signs and others do not. Some people only see some of the signs. In order to see a sign or to receive a message you have to believe in an afterlife and that once people cross over they can still communicate with you. Once you start believing, suddenly a whole new world opens up to you and you start seeing signs and receiving messages all the time. There are many benefits to receiving these signs and messages. You will realize that life continues after death and that you will be with your friends and family once again. You will realize that this life is not a one time event but instead that you continue to develop spiritually even after you die. Once I came to understand and believe this truth, it took a large weight off of my shoulders as I realized that I did not have to get it totally right this time around. All I have to do is my best to live this life and to develop as much spiritually as possible. This brought me a lot of peace and allowed me to focus on my life's purpose which was to help other people as much as I can and to love myself despite all of my short comings. Today more than ever, people are often looking for help, guidance and healing in their lives but are struggling to find it. They often look to make contact with their deceased loved ones for help and healing. I often see people wanting readings or advice, many of them hoping to connect with a loved one who has passed. What they do not understand is that they do not need a medium to make that connection. It is true, that to begin with, a medium can help make that connection between loved one and spirit. When a person begins to believe in the intuition they were born with they become open to the possibilities of directly communicating with them. Spirits will take care of the rest and begin to communicate directly with them.

Spirits are constantly trying to connect with us. They leave messages or signs everywhere. They do this in numerous ways, for example with images, songs, feathers, dreams, and coins are often considered signs from spirit. My mother-in-law Fay has a habit of finding dimes in the most unusual places. She has also found far more dimes than the average person. To her, finding a dime, has always meant that her husband Bernie was sending her a message that he loved her and was still with her. My wife would often have lights flicker in our house unexpectedly, which she often took as a sign from her father-in-law Art who we all called Poppa, that he was there with us. This almost always happened around Christmas time and so when the lights on the decorations began to flicker we would always say, "Looks like Papa is here for Christmas!" Not everyone picks up on these types of messages. Usually their logical mind may cause them to dismiss the signs as nothing or simply a coincidence. Not all those on the other side communicate in the same manner. Some come through so clearly that, I immediately can sense their essence or spirit. I can tell who they were, what they did and how they felt about nearly everything. However sometimes it is not so easy and getting information about them is like trying to pull teeth. Sometimes the images or information that I get means nothing to the person receiving the message and so I have to look at the information differently. Sometimes the image or information is symbolic or sometimes the spirit will bring up memories or situations that happened or are happening in my life that allow me to understand, what their message is. For example, imagine I am having trouble getting information about a spirit and suddenly I see an image of my maternal grandfather. At first I wonder why all of a sudden my grandfather is showing up during the reading but after awhile I figure out that the spirit that is coming through for my client was their maternal grandfather also and so by association I am able to identify what the client's connection is to the spirit. If I am flashed a vision of my own dad when I am channeling a client's father from the other side, that spirit might also have the same name as my dad, Art or Arthur. Sometimes, it means instead that the client's dad and my dad had something else in common. Perhaps they both loved to play cards. Half the challenge is to figure out what spirit is giving you. It is like playing detective sometimes. Everything, means something. It is our job as mediums to figure out a different way to look at the evidence that spirit gives us if it is not obvious. In order to figure out the subtleties of mediumship you must devote time to studying and practice. There are many reasons to study mediumship but I do it for two main reasons. First of all it allows me to continue to develop spiritually and secondly if allows me to fulfill my spiritual destiny by helping and healing others. I have learned many things so far on my journey about what makes me the best medium I can be.

WHY IS THERE A FOX ON THE COVER OF THE BOOK?

This is a very good question. If you are reading this book then you probably have some intuitive gifts. So why do you think there is a fox on the cover of the book? To find out for sure you will have wait a bit.

WHAT ARE YOUR GIFTS AND HOW LONG HAVE YOU HAD THEM?

Well looking back on it now I guess I have always had certain gifts. I knew that growing up I was a "sensitive boy" and later a "sensitive man" but it was not until lately that I realized I have always been an empath.

WHAT IS AN EMPATH?

Empath is the root word for the word empathy which really means sensitive or caring. As an empath you care deeply about all living things. You can feel their emotions but especially their pain. You tend to have your feelings hurt quite easily and you really are impacted by what other people think and say about you. You are a pleaser and want everyone to like you. You can be an easy target and are often bullied, sometimes physically but most often emotionally. Empaths are extra sensitive so they are often very good at reading the energy of living things. Unless empaths learn how to ground themselves they often keep the negative energy of others inside and this can lead to depression or in the long term to chronic pain. Empaths are often very self reflective and this can lead to self esteem and self love issues. In relationships they are often more giving of love than their partners. On the bright side they are great healers, psychics and mediums.

WHAT IS A GOOD WAY TO GROUND YOURSELF?

H ere is a meditation I say to myself or listen to by playing a recording of it.

"Imagine a beautiful divine light shining down upon your head. As you breathe in, you breathe in this divine light which brings your body regeneration and rejuvenation. Focus on your breathing. When you breathe in, breathe in all of your energy that is out in the universe. All the energy that you have given to other people. All your energy that has been taken by other people. Bring your energy home, to the centre of your body. Now take three deep breaths and bring it all back. Now continue to breathe in the divine light as you focus on your exhale. On the breath out, imagine you are breathing out all the negative energy in your body. All the negative energy you have collected from other human beings. As well as any negative energy or blockages that have been lingering inside you for some time. Let them all go, this is your time, your space. No cares, no worries. Let them all go. Surrender to the all powerful creative force of the universe. Let that negative energy flow down and out of your body. Down into the ground, down to the centre of the earth. Where it is all destroyed. Focus on this release for your next three breaths. From the top of your head to the tips of your toes you feel perfect in every way. Perfect physically, perfect mentally, emotionally calm and serene. With every breath you take let yourself become more and more grounded."

Other things that you can do that help you become grounded are practicing mindfulness, meditating and taking walks in nature. Try them all and see which works best for you.

WHAT IS THE BEST WAY TO MEDITATE?

Meditation is a very hard practice to define because it can mean many different things for many different people. For me, meditation is basically sitting or lying very quietly. I usually focus on my breathing but once I have quieted my mind I try not to think about anything but instead to just try to become acutely aware of all my senses. I try to meditate roughly at the same time and in the same place each time. By doing this I feel it is easier to slip from meditation to mediumship. I think this happens because by meditating at the same time and in the same place spirits know when and where I will be available to make a connection with. I feel that spiritual energy builds up in that place over time and it becomes easier and easier to make connections with the spirit world. Before long, you will find that your spirit helpers are already there waiting for you as you sit down for meditation. I also use this time to connect with my spirit guides and spiritual advisors. This allows me to ask them for advice and to allow them to guide me on my spiritual journey. I love this quiet, private time. Here are a couple of suggestions if you are interested in trying meditation. I have created a webpage where I have recordings of a variety of guided meditations. A guided meditation is a recording where someone walks you through what to do. Sometimes it is accompanied with music, sometimes not. If you go to www.alfromcanada.com/meditations you can see a variety of sample meditations from famous authors. If you are just beginning I would suggest trying the one created by Adyashanti to start with as it is the most straight forward. Sonia Chouquette also creates beautiful meditations set to music. Finally, if you find you still are not sure if you are meditating properly you can always invest in a meditation device by the Muse company which is a headset that you wear on your head. It has sensors that can monitor your brainwaves. When you are meditating properly you will hear no sounds on the earphones and if you are really quieting your mind then you will hear birds chirping. However if your mind is distracted or active then you will hear the sound of a thunderstorm. What this device does is it gives you immediate feedback as to how you are doing. It allows you to adjust what you are doing until you are meditating more effectively. I found this very useful to begin with but once I figured out what was the best way for me to meditate I no longer needed it. The one draw back to this device is that it is a bit costly. Meditation increases your awareness of and sensitivity to the subtle, gentle presence of the spirit people. Daily meditation leads to greater self-understanding.

Meditation also teaches you to keep your mind focused. This is an essential skill for a good medium because the messages from spirit are often brief, and you might miss some of them if you cannot hold your focus.

WHAT OTHER GIFTS DO YOU THINK YOU HAVE?

In hindsight, believe I have always been very intuitive. At the time, when I was younger, I might not have known it but I remember always having "gut feelings" about certain decisions I had to make or a sense of alertness and awareness in certain dangerous situations. Little did I know, that my "gut feeling" was my natural psychic ability, which is sometimes called intuition. It is a gift that allows you to receive help from the spirit world in order to help guide you in your earthly spiritual journey. Intuition is a sense of knowing, and this knowing comes from within. This sense of knowing is spontaneous and happens automatically. If you try too hard to be intuitive, you will only make it more difficult for yourself. Intuition is not something that you can make happen. It just happens. It is one of your human characteristics, although unfortunately not everyone pays attention to their intuition.

How were you able to develop so quickly?

There are two other main reasons that helped me in my development. First of all I became a registered clinical hypnotherapist and probably the most important thing that happened to me was that after fifty-five years I finally began to believe in an after-life. Strangely, both of these reasons are closely related. In hindsight now, I think that I have always had psychic abilities, but it was not until I started believing in an after-life that the mediumship began. Prior to that I had been a very vocal sceptic of all new age thinking. My mother and daughter had very much been into "New Age" ideas and I had been tolerant but did not really believe in most of what they were learning.

My belief in an afterlife began when I became a registered clinical hypnotherapist. At the time I was working at a private boarding school and they paid for my training and certification so I could work as a counsellor and sports psychologist for the school. During my training I was hypnotized many times and learned how to overcome my logical mind's disbelief of the process. Later this really helped with mediumship as well. I often find that beginners have a real problem in believing that what they are doing is real. As mentioned earlier their logical mind prevents them from going beyond a very simple phase of their mediumistic development. So after two years, of working daily as a registered clinical hypnotherapist I decided to do some professional development in the area of "Past Life Regression Therapy". I happened to read a book by Michael Newton called, Journey of Souls. In this book a psychiatrist tells of how he used "Past Life Regression Therapy" in his daily practice. One day while working with a patient he was interrupted just when his patient had come to the part about her death in the past life that she was recalling under hypnosis. When he returned Newton forgot where he was in the session and asked his patient, "What happened next?" and his patient went on to describe what happened after the death and all about the journey to the after-life and what happened there. Newton was surprised but intrigued, so he started recording his sessions and including what he called the" life after life" question to all his past life sessions. After more than a thousand cases he found most of them were very similar and he wrote his book describing his findings. I was fascinated with his descriptions of the afterlife so after reading the book, I began to believe in an afterlife and very shortly after that is when my mediumship began.

As you have probably figured out by now, one requirement when it comes to being able to receive signs from the other side is that you have to believe in an afterlife. Another important factor to developing quickly is to practice as much as possible. Finally your development will happen much more quickly and your practice will be much more purposeful if you study under the guidance of a caring and talented mentor. I have been very lucky to have had Reverend Malcom Gloster as my mentor. He was perfect for me. It is important to find the right person to be your mentor. They have to understand you and to be able to communicate with you in a way that you can understand. At times they need to be forceful in order to push you out of your comfort zone. They also have to give honest feedback so you can learn from your mistakes. In my case he needed to be open-minded and tolerant because I liked to try so many non-traditional and new ways of mediumship. Malcolm is all these things and more. He is my mentor and one of my best friends. If you are looking for a mentor please contact me and I will help you find one.

How did you discover your gifts?

A few years ago after a family crisis, my wife Holly and I were devastated. We tried some counselling, but we did not think that it helped very much. Our daughter, Lauren, and my wife decided to try going to an intuitive circle and Holly found this to be very helpful as she was able to get advice and messages from her spirit guides. The following week, Lauren had gone home, and Holly asked if I would go to the circle with her. I agreed and so we went. It was held by a psychic-medium called Linda Pynacker and the night I went, there were about eight ladies and myself at the meeting. I read and agreed to a waiver that she asked me to sign which required that I have an open mind and to participate when I felt I had something to say. Linda started with a guided meditation where we were walking in a forest and we met an animal that had a message for us. In my case it was a Fox. Remember the cover of the book? Then we walked a little further and met one of our spirit guides. In my case it was my main spirit guide, a rather Roman looking man in a chariot with a long latin name which I could not pronounce so we decided I could call him Randy. We continued on further and met a loved one who had passed on. In my case it was my Mom.

Once the meditation was over we all took a few moments to write down what we remembered on a pad of paper. Afterwards we took turns reading our journey details out loud to the group. While we were reading Linda would give us additional insights as to what our images represented. Anyone else in the circle was encouraged to jump in and give their insights into what they thought each person's images meant as well. Well, suddenly I was picking up on everyone's readings and by the end of the night I was talking as much or more than Linda. While I was doing this Holly kept giving me strange looks. Afterwards she said to me, "Who are you?" and "What are you trying to do, be a smart ass and make fun of the whole evening?" I said, "No, I was just doing what I was told!!" Although it was an amazing night I was really confused, so later that week I had a private session with Linda to find out what was going on. She explained that I had been given a special gift and that often a person's psychic abilities are not revealed until they have gone through some personal challenge or drama. She also explained that I was not a clairvoyant but in fact a clairsentient. This was a new term to me which I found out means I get my messages through using feelings and empathy. This is how my journey began.

WHAT WERE SOME OF YOUR INITIAL SPIRIT CONTACTS LIKE?

One of my very first visits from the spirit world happened with the maternal side of the family. When I relaxed and began to meditate, I had a clear image of my cousin Jack who had passed away a few years before. I was laying on my bed meditating when I saw a picture of him in my mind. It was like he appeared in a dream. He wanted me to know that he was doing alright. I thanked him for all the things he had done for me when I was younger. I also apologized for some hard feelings that were created while we were playing softball in a small town near where we lived. He wanted me to tell my sister, Mary Ann and my brother Richard that he loved them as his brother and sister and that he was doing ok. He wanted to thank Richard for speaking at his funeral. He wanted me to tell Grace, his wife, and his family that he was ok. He then introduced his brother Jim, also my cousin, and passed me over to him.

Jim said he was doing alright. He had died in a tragic way but wanted to communicate that he was in a good place now and that his wife, Kathy, was also in a good place but they were not together. I thanked him for being like a big brother to me when I was growing up. He wanted me to tell his children that he and their mom were doing well.

That they should not feel guilty. What happened had nothing to do with them. That he had been in a bad place when he died and that he was not thinking about them or anything else when the tragic event happened. He felt terrible about how things ended. He loves them and is very proud of them.

At that point my uncle Bob jumped in. We talked about our relationship. We apologized to each other for our disagreements over the years then he asked me to tell his sons, Roger and Donald that he was sorry that he was not a better, more normal, father. He had in later life revealed that he was homosexual and regretted the rifts that caused in the family. He wanted them to know he loves them and really loves his grandchildren. He also wanted them to know that he thinks they are great fathers.

Lastly, my Uncle John came to me. He wanted me to make amends with his son David. David, my cousin, and I had a falling out a long time ago. I told him I would try but I could not promise anything. Then I looked up and there was a long line of relatives from that side of the family waiting to give me a message. I remember saying to them "Don't you guys have someone on your side of the family who can do this for you?" I told them they would have to wait for another time that I was too tired to do any more. Over the years most of my family have come through at some time or the other.

What is the difference between clairvoyance and clairsentience?

Clairvoyance is when a medium receives mental messages from spirit in the form of pictures. It literally means "clear seeing." Clairsentience is when a medium receives messages from spirit through the sense of feeling. Mediums who are very strong at giving clairsentient messages are very good at sensing what emotions the spirit is feeling now and what they felt in their earthly existence. Clairsentience literally means "clear sensing".

ARE THERE OTHER "CLAIRS"?

The other "clairs" include: Clairaudience which literally means "clear hearing". It is when a medium receives mental messages through the sense of hearing. They hear the spirit talk, or sing, or hear songs or sayings. Clairalience literally means "clear smelling" and is when a medium receives messages through the sense of smell. The medium can smell the perfume the spirit used to wear or the smell of the spirits favourite dinner cooking. Clairgustance, literally means, "clear tasting" and is when the medium receives messages through the sense of taste. For example the medium can taste the beer that a spirit used to drink. There is also Claircognizance which literally means, "clear knowing" and is when a medium is able to instantly receive all the information about a spirit all at once.

Not all mediums immediately have access to all the "clairs". To begin with they are usually stronger with one or two of them. For the longest time I was unable to receive messages by hearing or by using clairaudience. Then suddenly one day I heard a spirit's favourite song playing in my head followed by one of the spirit's favourite sayings. Now I get those kind of messages regularly. If you are frustrated because you are not able to make use of one or more of the clairs, please be patient. If you are meant to receive these types of messages then spirit will help you to develop them when the time is right. Please do not feel you are a failure because you are unable to use all the clairs. Many professional mediums use only two or three "clairs" and are still able to give amazing, life changing readings. Remember the best way for you to give messages is by doing it your way. Use whatever skills you have to become the best medium you can be at that time.

Did you start doing mediumship readings for people right away?

Initially, I focused on doing psychic readings using an oracle card deck. Just after my initial breakthrough I visited a new-age book store and starting looking at all the different tarot and oracle decks.

The one that spoke to me the loudest, was John Holland's green deck called "Sacred Tarot of the Heart". I was drawn to this deck because of the beautiful artwork and pictures. I began pulling cards and doing readings for all my family and friends. I never read the book that came with this deck and I removed the Chakra cards while doing readings because that was what worked best for me. Every time I did a reading for someone it was always different even if I drew the same card for two different people. I allowed myself to focus on the first thing in the card that drew my attention to it. Sometimes it was the border colour of the card, another time it was the number at the top, sometimes it was the words at the bottom but most of the time it was something in the picture itself. It seemed like the card was giving me a hint or was acting as a guide post to help me focus on what to say to the person I was reading for. Then I let my intuition fill in the rest. I am sure I was using my claircognizant skills because I just seemed to know what to say. I quickly moved from reading a single card to having the client draw three cards. I used a three card spread called "Past, Present and Future". In this spread the first card gave me insight into their past, the second card their present and the third card their future. I also found that the number at the top of the card usually represented some sort of time frame. So if the number at the top was a six then I knew the time frame for the card was either six years, six months, six weeks, or six days and again I would say this out loud to the client and as I did this I could tell which one was correct. I again used my claircognizance skills to just know which time frame was the correct one at that particular time. I do not know why but I felt really comfortable using the cards, it seemed so natural to me. The psychic readings came very easily to me and still do to this day. Often the key to a psychic reading is sensing the energy of the person that is sitting in front of you. Sometimes it is sensing the energy of a spirit of the person receiving a reading and sometimes it is sensing both their energies. The cards just give me a hint or point me in the right direction when giving a reading. I can just as easily give a psychic reading without cards or with tea leaves or photographs or some other way if necessary. I encourage you to try as many different ways of doing a psychic reading as possible, for by doing this, you can begin to figure out where your strengths lie. Remember the only right way to do a reading is the one that works best for you.

What is the difference between psychic readings and mediumship?

A psychic reading is done for a living person where you give insights into a person's life, situation and some hints or insights into their future. I believe that all humans have free will, so their future is not set in stone but can change over time based on the decisions they make. Mediumship is communication with a spirit who has passed on. A handy saying to remember this is the following saying: "A medium is always a psychic but a psychic is not always a medium!" I am lucky and have both abilities.

How did you make the transition from psychic to mediumship readings?

Within a month of the dawning of my gifts, I began going to a local Spiritualist Church. I remembered that in a Spiritualist Church service they perform mediumship to help prove the existence of an afterlife. Fortunately we had a local spiritualist church called The Cowichan Valley Spiritualist Church of Healing and Light. I met Reverend Patrica Gunn there who was their leader and the person who created this church over thirty years ago. I was amazed to watch real platform mediumship every Sunday during the church services. After one session, I asked Patricia about mediumship training and she invited me to attend her personal mediumship development circle which was held every Thursday night. This was exactly what I needed to begin my mediumship training. During this time I read many helpful books whose reviews you can read about on my web site at www.alfromcanada.com. One of the most beneficial techniques I learned is called "Sitting in Spirit" or sometimes "Sitting in the Power".

What is "Sitting in the Power"?

Sitting in Spirit" or "Sitting in the Power" is a term used to describe using meditation to expand your personal energy sometimes called your auric field, in order to raise your vibrational energy. In order to sit in the power I begin meditating and start focussing on my breathing. After awhile I switch my focus from my breathing to concentrating on the energy field or auric field that surrounds my body. I imagine that with each breath I draw in, that I am receiving Divine spiritual energy and then on the exhale I imagine as I am breathing out that I am breathing this divine energy right into my energy field causing it to expand. I continue to do this until I feel my energy field fills up the room I am meditating in. Then I imagine my energy field fills up my entire house, then the entire neighbourhood, then the whole town, then the country, then the earth, then the universe. By doing this I feel it builds my own energy field and allows me to connect with spirits more easily. By doing this exercise I become more aware of my energy field and I can also begin to sense when a spirit's energy enters my field. This helps me quickly and easily connect with them. I also feel that this exercise allows me to raise my vibrational energy.

WHY WOULD YOU WANT TO RAISE YOUR VIBRATIONAL ENERGY?

Quantum physics has found that everything in life has its own spiritual energy that resonates at different frequencies. Spirits are no different, even though they have no physical body, their spirit continues to vibrate at a very high resonance. As a medium you need to raise your vibrational energy level so that you can match and connect with the spirit's vibrational energy level in order to connect with them and to begin giving the reading. There are many ways to raise your vibrational energy level. Again try as many different ways as you can to increase you vibrational energy so you can to find out what works best for you. There is an excellent book written by Kyle Gray called "Raise your Vibration". He has a lot of activities in his book that you may want to try.

WHAT DO YOU DO TO RAISE YOUR VIBRATIONAL ENERGY?

I have found that listening to fast classical Rock n Roll music is the quickest and best way to raise my vibrational energy. It is always quite amusing to me to watch my colleagues before a psychic fair. Usually the mediums at a psychic fair get together about 15 minutes before the fair opens to the public and say an opening prayer. Then they go to their tables and begin to raise their vibrational energy by "sitting in spirit". All the other mediums usually sit very quietly in meditation preparing themselves for the reading to come. Then there is me, sitting with headphones on listening to my special playlist of music that gets me psyched up. I am often dancing in my chair. I always seem to be the odd ball, the one sticking out from the crowd. However, this is what works best for me and so that is why I do it. Music can raise your vibrational energy and cut through any negativity you are experiencing. For me, listening to fast rock n roll music always raises my vibrational energy. It reminds me of when I used to listen to warm up music to get ready to play in basketball games. You should try as many ways as you can until you find what method works best for you.

How does a mediumship reading work?

There are usually two parts to giving a message from spirit. Usually, there is the giving evidence followed by the giving of a message from spirit. In the first part of a reading a medium makes a connection with a spirit and begins to share what they receive in order to help the client figure out who the spirit is. Ideally the client should only answer yes, no, or I do not know in response to the evidence given. For example, the medium might say, "I have a tall man here who is dressed in a three piece suit wearing a tall black top hat that looks like the one that Abraham Lincoln might have worn. Does this make any sense?" If the client can picture who it is the medium is talking about they might say, "Yes, I can take that". Then the medium would continue to give pieces of evidence until the client was totally sure they knew which spirit was coming through. Once it has been established which spirit is coming through by sharing enough evidence with the client, then it is time to move onto the message. For example, "The reason this spirit is coming through today is to tell you that they love you and that they are sorry about how they treated you upon their death bed."

For a medium this process is often like doing detective work or like playing charades because you do not always get clear evidence from the spirit. Sometimes it is like trying to describe a scenic picture while looking through a foggy window. It is important to only give what you get. Your logical mind will want to try to figure it out and to interpret what it means. It is important to only give what you get and let the client decide what the significance is. For example, one time I was giving a reading and the first image I received was a cow. My logical mind immediately began thinking, "Well this is stupid, no one is going to take this, if you give this evidence then you will look like a total failure and fraud." Fortunately, I gave what I got by saying, "It is funny, but spirit is showing me a cow" does that mean anything to anyone? Out of an audience of about forty, one person raised their hand. It turns out that she had a young grandchild who they called, "Moo" and this was the perfect bit of evidence for me to begin my reading with.

How does a medium connect with spirit?

When mediums connect with the spirit people, they are in an altered state of awareness. So if you want to connect with the spirit people, you will have to learn to shift your awareness out of your ordinary consciousness and into the mediumistic state of consciousness. This is done by raising your vibrational energy and by setting your intention to connect with spirit.

Begin by setting an intention that you are going to connect with the spirit world. I imagine flipping that switch that turns on a neon light inside my head that says, "Open for business!" I mentally switch it on by saying an opening prayer to ensure that my connection is from the most positive and high sources and that the messages I get are the best for all concerned. Once I have done this I know that anything that comes to me in the form of an image, a sound, a feeling or a thought comes directly from spirit and that it comes for a reason and is part of the reading.

For some mediums, the opening prayer alone is not enough to achieve this state. I know several mediums who purposefully empty their minds and hearts of all of their own personal concerns before they can connect with a spirit. Some people imagine a box in a closet where they put all their stresses and worries into. Sometimes mediums begin the process of mediumship by taking a couple of deep, relaxing breaths. I suggest you find your trigger or starting routine and then keep it as simple as possible. There is no need to have an elaborate or complicated trigger, because eventually you will not need a trigger at all because you will just automatically be able to connect with spirit at will.

WHAT HAPPENED NEXT IN YOUR DEVELOPMENT?

Once I was receiving messages from spirit it seemed like I was open 24/7 to any spirit who has been waiting to give a message to their loved ones. I did not know what to do and thought I might be going crazy until at circle I was taught about setting boundaries with spirits.

How do you set boundaries with spirits?

Mediums are naturally sensitive, so you must be mindful of the energies that you send out into the world, because what you send out will eventually come back to you. Mediums are easily affected by the discord and disharmonious conditions in their lives. I always set boundaries while dealing with spirits. They know that unless I have done my opening prayer and turned my switch on saying "Open for business!", I am not to be contacted by them. You can also turn your switch to off if you need to end your connection with a spirit, any time you wish. Remember you are in control.

WHAT ELSE HELPED YOU WITH YOUR DEVELOPMENT?

The two other things that really helped me with my development in the beginning were keeping a success journal and automatic writing.

WHAT IS A SUCCESS JOURNAL?

I found that when my mediumship gifts were discovered that it was so incredible that I felt I should write down everything that happened and so I took to writing down my readings. Once I started doing this a most amazing thing happened. When I started to write my readings down I suddenly started to receive more evidence and more powerful messages. When I did some research I found out this was called automatic writing.

WHAT IS AUTOMATIC WRITING?

Automatic writing can also be described as divine writing. It is writing that is inspired and in some cases dictated by spirit. One of the best examples of automatic writing are the books channeled by Louise Hays from the ascended master Abraham. Other examples of inspired or automatic writings are the works of Edgar Cayce and White Feather. A similar experience happens during a spiritualist church service when the minister does inspired speaking.

WHAT IS INSPIRED SPEAKING?

Inspired speaking is when spirit speaks through a medium to provide inspirational messages to audiences of more than one person. This commonly happens during a Spiritualist Church service when the minister gives an unprepared talk based upon the reading. They trust that spirit will come through and use their voice to give the message. Often their voice will sound different and they will speak faster than normal.

WHEN DID YOU BECOME AN INTERMEDIATE LEVEL MEDIUM?

I knew I had advanced enough to call myself an intermediate level medium when my focus changed from my own personal learning and development and began shifting to doing psychic and mediumship readings for other people. For me this signalled the moment when I transitioned from a beginner to an intermediate medium.

As an intermediate level medium I began to believe that our purpose on earth is to assist and serve humanity and that my purpose as a medium is to bring healing by providing evidence of the survival of consciousness beyond physical death. I realized that as long as my motivation for mediumship is to be an instrument for Spirit and to help others, that my gift would continue to unfold and that the Divine would support my efforts.

Mastering Mediumship

Book 2 - Intermediate   **Albert Olson**

WHEN DO YOU BECOME AN INTERMEDIATE MEDIUM?

As a beginning medium you are discovering your gifts and you are learning all about how they affect you. You are also finding out what is the best way to use your gifts. Really it is an explorative and learning period. A period of self-discovery. As you become more self-confident and gain some experience you slowly move towards becoming an intermediate medium. When you are ready to do readings for other people and to shift your focus to helping and healing other people, this is when you become an intermediate medium. It is also a shift from predominately psychic readings to a better balance of psychic and mediumship readings.

WHAT ALLOWED YOU TO BEGIN TO DO READINGS FOR OTHER PEOPLE?

In order to begin doing readings for other people I had to develop confidence in my own abilities. I was very keen to start experimenting and trying new things so it was only natural that I would begin to try out my skills in the real world. I continued to go to my original development circle but I also started going to another circle run by another one of the local Spiritualist Church's mediums. So I was going to the Spiritualist Church on Sundays, circle on Monday and Thursday nights. In between I was reading as many books about mediumship as possible. Two of the most helpful books that really were written with mediumship development in mind were: "Where Two Worlds Meet" written by Janet Nohavec and "Mediumship Mastery" by Stephen Hermann. They were extremely helpful because they were specifically written to help people develop their mediumship. They gave great ideas and activities that were fun to try either by yourself or with a group of friends. After reading these books I was really keen to try out these new techniques by doing readings for people.

Describe your first "real" mediumship readings?

The most important lesson I learned from my early readings was that I could actually make a connection with spirit. That I actually could be a medium. I started by giving readings to my friends and family. I chose people that would support or at least humour me as I tried my hand at my new craft. I started with my wife and kids but then moved onto more challenging people. My older brother Richard was a good example. Richard was a very practical and logical person and he always made fun of our mother whenever she talked to him about her latest "new age" book that she was reading. He thought she was wasting her time. So when our grandfather came through to me one night while I was meditating and asked me to give Richard a message from him I was really dumbfounded. I wanted to do what my grandfather asked but I knew that as soon as I brought it up with my brother that he would think I was crazy. It took a few days for me to build up the courage but eventually I gave him a call and told him that I suddenly had these new gifts and that I was able to talk to spirits. He was very quiet and I could tell that he was skeptical. I then went on to tell him that our grandfather Twain had a message for him. He said, "Yeah, what's that?" I said that grandfather wanted to tell him that he loved him like a son and that he would be there when Richard crossed over. All Richard said was, "Oh, that's nice." And then he changed the subject. I did not know what to think until the day when our sister Mary Ann called me and said she just had a call from Richard who told her. "I think Albert is going crazy." Thanks a lot Grandad, I thought. But then a funny thing happened . Within a month Richard was diagnosed with dementia and when he told Mary Ann about it he said, "But it is ok because when I cross over I know that Grandfather will be there to meet me." I nearly fell over. Then shortly after that Richard and I were driving somewhere and he said to me, "What have Jack and Bob been up to?" He was referring to our cousin Jack and uncle Bob who were both deceased. I looked at him to see if he was teasing me, but when I realized that he was serious I told him all about my many visits with Jack and Bob. Later that year my beautiful brother Richard, the skeptic, gave me the most incredible gift. He paid for me to go to England and to attend Arthur Findlay College so that I could refine my mediumship skills. Later as his dementia became worse I often took Richard to different support groups and he would always introduce me as his brother Albert, the medium.

It was after many such successful experiences giving readings to family that I became brave enough to give reading in person to the public. One of the first times this happened was when our local Spiritualist Church held a spirit fair to raise funds for the church. At the spirit fair the mediums of the church give half hour readings to the public. I was honoured when they asked me to join them. I gave about a dozen readings and all the feedback was very positive. After that I was no longer concerned about giving readings to others. I think the main reason I was able to begin doing public one on one mediumship readings was that I was able to overcome several fears that were blocking me from making the connections I needed to give a successful reading.

WHAT FEARS WERE BLOCKING YOUR PROGRESS?

In hind sight I realize that I had many fears that at different times blocked my progress. They included the fear of ridicule, the fear of failure, the fear of "evil spirits", and the fear of making things up.

What do you mean by fear of ridicule?

At some point all aspiring mediums will have to overcome the fear of ridicule or the fear of "coming out". I was embarrassed to tell my brother about my mediumship because I was afraid that he would tease me publicly or at family celebrations. I was afraid of what the people in my life would think of me. I was still working as a school teacher at the time for a very conservative private school and I was not sure how they would feel about me going public. However, at some point if you want to advance to becoming an advanced or professional medium you will have to let the world know that you are a medium. There will definitely be both good and bad consequences of going "public". There will be those who are truly excited for you and will be keen to get a reading and to learn all about your journey but there will also be those who will be sceptical and think you are crazy. It is very hard to be the best medium you can be if you do not have a supportive community to fall back on. I have been blessed that my wife has always believed in me and has been very supportive. However, some family members have not been quite so kind. For example one of my wife's cousins who she has always been very close to has had a very hard time accepting the changes I have gone through. He is a very smart and logical person who has never accepted any type of religion in his life. Perhaps it would be best to describe his religion as a belief in science. He insists he needs to see the proof before he will believe in anything. When I asked him what type of

proof he needed, he quoted Carl Sagan who once said, "Extraordinary claims require extraordinary evidence!" My response to him should have been to respond with the following quotes by Carl Sagan:

"Somewhere, something incredible is waiting to be known" or

"Absence of evidence is not evidence of absence." In his case I do not think there will ever be enough evidence to change his mind. So I was faced with a decision. Do I try to convince him or just not talk to him any more. Fortunately, we both valued our friendship so much that we were are able to agree to disagree about mediumship and we just do not talk about it any more.

Another example of a relationship that was strained by my becoming a medium was with our former son-in-law. Unfortunately this time the relationship ended with hurt feelings. Our daughter lived with this man for eight years in a common-law relationship. For many of these years they lived in New Zealand. We loved Aaron as if he were one of the family. We were very sad when their relationship ended and they both went their own ways. We stayed in touch with Aaron and celebrated his birthday and other holidays each year. We were very happy when he found a new partner and fell in love. They married and soon after had a baby boy. We were still actively involved in Aaron's life and spent a lot of time with his son. We often babysat for them when his wife went back to work. Then suddenly, Aaron's wife no longer wanted us in their life anymore. My wife and I were very hurt because we had become very close to their son and thought of ourselves as surrogate grandparents. Eventually Aaron came to talk to us and said that his wife no longer wanted us around because of my mediumship. She came from a conservative Christian background and was afraid that I was dealing with the "dark side" and did not want me to influence their son. This really hurt. My wife cried every night for several weeks and I felt really guilty because she really did not have anything to do with my mediumship. It was not her fault that we could no longer visit the boy. If only Aaron and his wife would have talked to me, I could have told them that I have never encountered an evil spirit and that what I do is help and heal people. My mediumship comes from a place of love. Unfortunately her upbringing did not allow her to overcome her worst fears.

If you have no one in your family who supports you it can be very difficult to be a medium unless you find another supportive community in person or online. My poor sister is a good example of a medium who has no support from her husband and very little support from her children. This is one of the reasons why I created a free online Mediumship Development Circle. It is a place that like minded-people can grow and develop and be supported on their journey without fear of judgement. For info on my free sessions go to my website at www.alfromcanada.com/zoom.

How did you overcome your fear of failure?

Well to be honest this was not a very big fear for me at all. For the most part I have always been very confident. Not having this fear has been both good and bad for me. It was good in that having confidence and pushing myself, helped me to progress quickly, but it was also bad in that it sometimes led people to think that I was arrogant. I remember early in my journey I was feeling that I really needed a mentor and at the time I was reading several books by Sonia Choquette. When I was just beginning, her books really spoke to me.

In one section in her book. "Trust Your Vibes" she tells how she approached the Dean of a university while applying for acceptance in to an overseas program. She told him that she really needed this placement because for her it was a "soul thing" and that as a result of her sharing her vulnerability, she was able to eventually be accepted into the program. Well, this really spoke to me, and so I reached out to her to see if she would consider being a mentor for me. I felt that mediumship was a "soul thing" for me. I was shocked when she eventually replied saying, "Why would I help someone that is as arrogant as you? What makes you think I would want to work with you? Do you know how many people write me about working with them because it is a "soul thing"? Talk about being shut down. So much for being vulnerable! My dream is one day we will work together at a conference or workshop and she can get to know the real me.

Sometimes my confidence causes people to feel threatened. I am the type of person who is a competitive extravert that likes to be the first to participate. As a boy in elementary school I often got in trouble for yelling out the answer to the teacher's questions before they could ask anyone else. I would like to think that I enjoy being the first to volunteer to do something because I am keen and excited but if I am honest there is a part of me that likes the recognition. I guess there is a part of me that likes to "show off". Although this can be very annoying to other participants or presenters it also keeps me very engaged and I always get the opportunity to try everything. I certainly am never afraid of failure.

An important key to overcoming the fear of failure is your attitude towards failure. For example if you are afraid that you will look stupid or that you are going to fail, then it is very hard to take the risk of trying anything that might have the slightest possibility of failure. This can really slow down how quick you progress as a medium. However, if you see failure as a positive experience that is part of learning then you are never afraid to try something. For example, I remember when I was first learning to play basketball in high school. I did not start playing until my grade eleven year so I had a lot of catching up to do to compete with the other boys trying out for the team. I remember that doing left hand layups as being very difficult for me because I was not used to using my non-dominant hand. I also remember that most players would try using their left hand in warm ups but in a game situation or scrimmage when they were faced with having to do a left hand lay up they almost always used their right hand and played it safe. Sometimes this worked for them but sometimes by using their right hand it allowed the defender to block their shot. I remember thinking that in a game or scrimmage I was going to use my left hand no matter what. In the beginning I missed most of those shots but I knew that eventually in a really important situation I was going to have to make that left hand layup under pressure and if I have never practiced it in a game situation that I would never have the confidence to make the shot. So in the beginning I missed most of my left hand layups and I was not a very valuable player to my team but two years later playing in the provincial championships I remember making a left hand layup in over time to help our team win. I was able to do this because by then it was second nature and automatic. So when it came to mediumship several decades later I was always keen to go first when doing mediumship in a circle or when I was taking courses at Arthur Findlay

College because I knew if I failed I would learn from it and that eventually I would have to do readings in front of a public audience. I remember thinking to myself that even on the days when I was tired or not feeling into it, that if I was asked by the circle leader if I wanted to do a reading I would always jump up and say yes because eventually I would have to give public readings when I might not be at my best. I just would not allow myself to pass or to not participate. An amazing thing happened as a result of this attitude. I found that I was able to give readings whenever I was asked because spirit always was there to help me. I learned to trust spirit to come through even if I had felt nothing initially or felt I was too tired to do a reading.

I found that having immediate positive reinforcement really helped me overcome any fear of failure. This is why I would highly recommend keeping a success journal as discussed earlier in this book. Also I found that doing pair readings when you are first starting out to be a very affirming way to build confidence.

WHAT ARE PAIRED READINGS?

Paired readings are when you do a mediumship reading with a partner. There are many advantages to doing readings this way. Two of the best mediums I know, Simon James and Bruce Robertson, work almost entirely together. Although independently they are both incredible mediums when they work together they are even more amazing. Simon and Brian are tutors at Arthur Findlay College and run their own church, The Open Door, in Victoria, British Columbia, Canada. I always use the analogy of tag team wrestling when I think of paired readings. In tag team wrestling you compete as a team of two. One wrestler begins the fight and when they get tired or hurt they can tag their partner by slapping hands and then their partner can come in the ring, fresh, and take over for awhile. The same is true in mediumship. You work with a partner, one of you starts a reading while the other connects with the same spirit. The first medium gives evidence until they need a break and then they hand off to their partner who continues to give evidence. The same routine applies to the message. One medium goes first and gives the message they are receiving and then the second medium follows with what they are picking up. The advantages to doing paired readings is that it takes the pressure off of having to be totally responsible for giving the evidence and message. Once you hand off the reading to your partner, it gives you a moment to catch your breath, refocus and to rebuild or strengthen your connection with spirit. Often when the other medium is giving evidence or the message, you will automatically be able to add small bits to what they are saying or to give more details to their evidence. Sometimes what they are saying leads you or directs you to a whole new line of evidence. In our Online Franciscan Spiritualist Church services I often do paired readings with my mentor Reverend Malcolm Gloster. I find this a very relaxing and successful way to do a reading. As a beginner it often helps to pair with a more experienced medium with whom you have rapport and who is supportive. Not all pairings are created equal and so you might have to try a few partners until you find the right one for you. I often use this technique as a mentor to help beginning mediums to increase their confidence.

WHAT ARE SOME OTHER WAYS TO BUILD CONFIDENCE?

There are many ways to build confidence such as: creating a success journal, using paper and pen when others are reading, piggy backing, practice, affirmations and finding different ways to connect. Again, I encourage you to try all these different strategies and find out which ones suit you best. We have already talked about keeping a success journal, diary or blog. By writing down all your successes it allows you to go back and look at your successes when you are having a rough patch and are feeling discouraged. Remember that good mediums do not go bad overnight. We can all have bad days or even a bad week. I am reminded of a line from the movie "Slaughterhouse Five" where the main character who is a time traveller, gets taken prisoner by a race from the future and is put on display for his captors to watch as if he was in a zoo. He becomes very sad and depressed. He is haunted by the negative experiences he remembers from earlier in his life. His captors tell him, "A good way to spend eternity is to concentrate on the good times". Mediumship is like this also. If you only remember the failures you will soon believe that you are not a worthwhile medium at all. Mediumship is like a glass half full of water, try to see your glass as half full rather than half empty. Concentrate on the good times, write down your successes and reread them when necessary.

www.alfromcanada.com/mediumship

Why should I use "paper and pen" while others are giving a reading?

I find this very helpful. When others are giving a reading I try to connect to the same spirit. I write down any evidence I get. If the evidence I wrote down comes up in the reading I give myself a "check mark" or a "gold star" next to it on the paper. This is a non-threatening way of getting positive feedback. If I have some check marks and I feel like I have connected to the same spirit then it allows me to ask questions after the reading of either the other medium or about their client or about the other information that I received. This is often called "piggy backing".

WHAT IS "PIGGY BACKING"?

"Piggy Backing" is like a pair reading but may involve more than just two mediums. This often happens during a development circle or during group practice. "Piggy Backing" is when you or a group of mediums adds to the reading of the initial medium. A medium starts and gives a reading and then other mediums join in to provide extra evidence or to augment the message. There is a certain protocol that is involved in "piggybacking". I never "piggyback" during a reading unless the medium who is doing the reading asks for help. If I am not asked and if I have something to add to the reading I will wait until the medium is finished their reading and then I will politely ask if it would be ok to add my insights. Then it is totally up to the original medium whether they want to let you join in. Sometimes the original medium will feel that their reading is complete and refuse your request or they may be happy to have you add your information. I always respect their decision because it was their reading initially.

WHERE CAN I FIND POSITIVE AFFIRMATIONS ABOUT MEDIUMSHIP?

There are many places to buy recordings of affirmations but very few if any of them deal specifically with mediumship. So I made my own. The best one I made was while I was attending Arthur Findlay College. In the evenings I would review what I learned during the day and then write my notes out as affirmations. The first affirmation would be in the third person, "You are an amazing medium". Then it was followed by the same affirmation in the first person, "I am an amazing medium". I liked this format because it is like a divine source is telling you your affirmation and then you repeat it to make it your own. You can find a copy of my recording of this set of affirmations at:

https://www.alfromcanada.com/affirmations-by-albert-olson.html.

WHAT ARE SOME DIFFERENT WAYS TO CONNECT?

There are just about as many ways to connect to spirit as there are mediums. In the end you will find the best way for you to connect. When I was starting out I found a few very useful ways to help me connect to spirit. Here are my five favourite ways to connect: Blank Screen, Open the Door, Long Hallway, Connecting with Spirit through Meditation, and Listening to fast music. With all these methods I close my eyes, and imagine that I am turning on a switch that lights up a big neon light that says, "OPEN FOR BUSINESS". This is my way of letting spirit know that I am open to receive messages. Suzanne Giesemann, a famous medium and mentor, would say that I am setting my intention to start work. Once I am open for business I now know that any form of message or thought that comes into my mind now comes from spirit and is part of the reading. What follows is a brief description of these methods.

WHAT IS THE "BLANK SCREEN" METHOD OF CONNECTING TO SPIRIT?

One way for me to connect once I have become "open for business" is to imagine that the back of my forehead is a large blank screen, or movie screen in a theatre. Any image or sound or feeling that I get while I watch this screen is part of my message from spirit. This method is particularly good for starting a reading and is especially good for clairvoyance.

WHAT IS THE "OPEN DOOR" METHOD OF CONNECTING TO SPIRIT?

This method was extremely helpful for me when I was first beginning. After becoming "open for business" I would imagine that I heard a knock at my front door. I would go to the door knowing that there was a spirit on the other side but not knowing anything about them. Then I would imagine that I opened the door and there they were. But the door only stays open for just a few seconds. In that time however I know everything I need to start giving my evidence. "It's a man, a tall man, dressed in a formal black suit with a grey vest and a tall black hat like Abraham Lincoln, etc,". It is amazing what you can get just from one short glance at someone. This method was an eye opener for me because prior to this I always thought that when I connected with spirit that I would continue to see them throughout the reading. Once I realized I only needed a glance to get my info then connecting became much less stressful.

WHAT IS THE "LONG HALLWAY" METHOD OF CONNECTING TO SPIRIT?

This method of connecting is reminiscent of doing a past life regression during hypnotherapy. After becoming "open for business" imagine you are suddenly in a long hallway with doors on each side. Each door represents a spirit that wants to connect with you. However, one door especially draws you toward it. It is speaking to you or calling to you. You can tell which door it is because it is lit up and light is shining out from underneath it. You approach the door and open it and step through. You are now back in the spirit's time and setting. You look around and use all your senses to get your bearings. Then from out of the fog the spirit approaches you and then begins to speak to you. Etc. This method allows you to use all of your senses and all of the "clairs" to gather evidence and to give your message. It is a more in depth method than the open door method. It is also a great meditation to use in circle to meet spirit guides, spirit animals and spirits from the other side.

What is the "meditating" method of connecting to spirit?

Another way to connect with spirit is to use a guided meditation. Here is a sample of one that I use with mediums I am mentoring.

Meditation for Mediumship

Continue to relax,

focus on your breathing,

and continue to send your love

to the spirit world.

With every breath you take

And every word I say

Allow your self to become more and more relaxed

More and more in tune with your body

Allow your body's vibrational energy to become higher and faster

Higher and faster

Higher and faster

Become more and more aware of the spirits around you

Allow them to come into sharper and sharper focus

as they begin to make their connection with you.

Allow your vibrational energy to fill the room

And as you do this you.

Will become aware

Aware that there is one spirit

One spirit in particular that really wants to connect with you.

This spirit is a very special spirit

A spirit that has come here today for a very specific reason.

Welcome them and thank them for coming.

Make clear your intention to connect with them.

Let them know that you intend to help them give their message.

And suddenly an amazing thing happens.

It is like you just switched your mediumship light switch to on.

A light switch that illuminates the sign that says

"Open for Business"

And now that you are open for business

Begin to notice what you sense and feel inside your own body.

Use your medical intuition to notice

To notice any physical sensations—

perhaps aches and pains—

or perhaps muscles that this spirit used often.

At the same time notice any feelings and emotions t

hat you are feeling.

106

Ask them to share their story with you.

Perhaps

They are sending love back to someone

or perhaps they are suddenly sending you a clue

A clue to pass on to someone

Someone who is here with us today.

Ask them for specific evidence

Detailed evidence that will allow them to be

recognized by the person they have come to visit.

Use your clairvoyance or your sense of sight to

notice if there are any visual impressions,

or thoughts,

or pictures,

that have drifted

into your mind's eye.

See them as if you have a blank screen

A blank screen right behind your eyelids

Right in your third eye.

Who knows what you will see

Do not try to find out why they have sent these images

Just give what you get

Perhaps you will see

a shared memory

A shared memory that they want to use to reminisce with their loved one.

Use your Clairaudience or your sense of hearing to

Pay attention to

any sounds that you hear

perhaps in your mind

perhaps in the room that you are sitting in.

Perhaps in your inner ear.

A favourite song,

Or

a type of music,

Or a saying

or type of saying they were likely to say.

Perhaps a joke or a pet name.

Perhaps you will hear a name

A name of some significance will be whispered into your inner ear.

Using Clairalience or the sense of smell

To notice if a fragrance now comes into your awareness

When it does

identify the smell.

See if you can smell the scent of cooking

Or a perfume or cologne

The smell of smoke or alcohol

Some smell that makes people think of this spirit

Now, using Clairgustance or your sense of taste

Identify any taste or tastes you have in your mouth.

Gently observe all that is going on in your body

and in your awareness.

Ask the spirit people to connect with you

Connect with you more closely than ever before

so that you can better perceive them.

Using your clairsentience or your sense of empathy/feeling try to get a

sense of this spirit's personality. Generally, were they happy or sad? do

they have any regrets?

do they have any thing they have left unsaid?

What is it that they desperately want to say today?

Now, ask them who they have come to give a message to?

Use your sense of claircognizance or your sense of knowing

to understand this spirit better and to realize who they are here for.

WHAT IS THE "FAST MUSIC" METHOD OF CONNECTING TO SPIRIT?

Finally I find, as I mentioned earlier that once I am "open for business", I really like to listen to fast rock and roll music. I find this raises my vibrational energy and I find that I make better and more numerous connections by doing this. During our Franciscan Spiritualist Church Service I am usually so busy running the service that I do not have time to think about mediumship so I like to listen to "Spirit in the Sky" by Norman Greenbaum or some other fast music from my playlist. It usually only takes a minute or two and I have several readings ready to go. As I mentioned earlier, for me it is like listening to warm up music before a basketball game. It gets me psychic up but also allows me to connect with spirit.

WHY IS THERE A FOX ON THE COVER OF ALL THE BOOKS IN THIS SERIES?

Near the beginning of my journey my wife, Holly and I went on a road trip to Prince George, British Columbia. One evening just after sunset we went out to West Lake to check out our old house. Just past the Provincial Camp Site we saw something coming down the road toward us. At first we thought it was a dog but as we went past it we realized it was a fox and he had a rabbit in his mouth. I thought this was too much of a coincidence as in my recent visualizations I had realized that the fox was indeed my spirit animal. He had come to me before in my meditations and now here he was in person. The funny thing is that in all the time we lived at West Lake we could not recall having ever seen a fox. This was no ordinary fox. It was a silver fox. When we passed him on the road he stopped and watched us. We backed up and he just sat there and stared at us. We were scrambling trying to get our camera and he started to run away. Holly said, "No wait, I want to get a picture" so he stopped and sat down again. Later, after we had visited our old house we came back and he was waiting for us again in the middle of the road. We had a good conversation and then said good bye. We felt like it was a message. We felt his message was: To be calm, not to be afraid, be brave and be patient, and do not run away. I love my spirit animal and I often sign my emails and messages with a fox symbol. This is why there is a picture of a fox on the cover of this book. Hands up, how many of you guessed correctly or simply knew why intuitively? Probably most of you.

WHAT WAS THE NEXT STEP IN YOUR DEVELOPMENT?

B esides continuing my own personal development, the next big step in my development was to begin providing my services to the general public through: Public Demonstrations, Psychic Fairs and Online Readings.

What do you mean by Public Demonstrations?

A public demonstration is a group of people that gather to watch a medium or a group of mediums do readings. There are paid demonstrations where people pay anywhere from strictly donations to hundreds or thousands of dollars to hear world famous mediums do readings. A public demonstration could be a simple gathering of friends and family who gather in someone's home and allows a medium or a developmental circle of mediums practice their skills in front of an audience for no charge. Or it could be someone like the Long Island Medium, Theresa Caputo, doing readings in front of a sold out arena of 5000 spectators each paying a minimum of $100 a seat. A public demonstration maybe a Spiritualist Church service where a medium does readings. This is often called platform mediumship. This type of mediumship could be as part of the service or it could be a church fundraiser where the church's mediums give readings for a small fee that gets donated to the church. In all of these examples, you are declaring yourself a medium and you will be under pressure to give readings in front of audiences that might have paid money to see you.

So public demonstrations are definitely a step further down the path in mediumship development.

WHAT IS A PSYCHIC FAIR?

A psychic fair is a gathering of mediums and other practitioners who gather in a central spot like a rented hall. Each person has their own table and people move around the tables to inspect the various things for sale and to get either psychic or mediumship readings. Sometimes a spiritualist church will hold a fundraiser where their mediums once again give readings and the proceeds go to the church. At a psychic fair the readings are usually in a one on one format. The medium is only giving one reading at a time to one person.

How did you start doing online readings?

I started doing online readings by joining Facebook and by joining certain Facebook groups where you are allowed to either advertise your services or to provide free readings for other people. A few of the best groups for developing mediums are: Mediumship 101 and Online Mediumship Development. Again, find a group that is right for you, where you are supported and where you feel comfortable. By joining several groups you can practice all day long if you want to.

WHAT WERE YOUR MOST SIGNIFICANT DEVELOPMENTS AT THIS TIME?

Without a doubt the biggest development for me, in so many ways was to attend Arthur Findlay College near London, England for two weeks.

WHAT IS ARTHUR FINDLAY COLLEGE AND HOW DID IT HELP YOU?

rthur Findlay College is the world's foremost college for the
advancement of spiritualism and the psychic sciences. Arthur
Findlay College, or Stansted Hall, was gifted to the Spiritualists '
National Union by J. Arthur Findlay, and in accordance with his wishes
is administered by the Spiritualists 'National Union as a College for
the advancement of Psychic Science. Arthur Findlay College offers
facilities unequalled anywhere in the world in the Spiritualist
movement as a residential centre where students can study Spiritualist
philosophy and religious practice, Spiritualist healing and awareness,
spiritual and psychic unfolding and kindred disciplines. Courses,
lectures and demonstrations are all offered by leading experts, together
with the additional features of a library, museum, lake, magnificent
grounds, recreational facilities and full board accommodation.

So almost exactly one year after discovering my gifts I made my
pilgrimage to Arthur Findlay College. Earlier in this book I told the
story of how my brother paid for me to attend this prestigious college.

All the spiritualist ministers, mediums and circle leaders that I had encountered had been to Arthur Findlay College and referenced their visits there as if it were a badge of honour. You were not really a "medium" or a "minister" until you had been to Arthur Findlay College for training. It meant that you had instant credibility and must know what you are talking about because you had been there. In fact no two visits are ever the same because they have many accredited teachers that they call "tutors" who teach a variety of courses a week at a time. You can find all their course offerings at: https://www.arthurfindlaycollege.org. At this point in my journey I had been to several workshops in my local area and even one in Vancouver British Columbia. I had always registered as a beginner and what I found after spending more than two thousand dollars on training was that often the presenters might have been very good mediums themselves but they were not professional teachers. So often the local workshops were poorly organized with very little interaction time and after awhile they became very repetitive. It seems like the workshop leaders had all learned how to present their information from the same source. Anyway I was really excited to go to Arthur Findlay College and to learn from the best tutors in the world. So then I had an agonizing decision to make. When should I go and whom should I learn from. There were many famous mediums giving courses that year. In the end, I cashed in all my airline points to buy a business class ticket

126

to London. It was not easy to find flights but eventually I found I could get flights in and out of Seattle through San Francisco to Copenhagen and then finally to London and back all in business class. With my ticket booked, I knew that I was going the last two weeks in June. Then I looked up Arthur Findlay College's calendar to see who I would be learning from. It turned out the first week was called a Master's week where you could choose from a variety of one or two day workshops from a variety of people. It was followed the next week by an Advanced course run by Val Williams. Then my logical mind kicked in, "What are you doing? You are going to spend your brothers money and all your airline points to attend Master and Advanced courses at Arthur Findlay College after being a medium for only one year? You must be crazy!" In the end I knew that this is exactly the experience that spirit had chosen for me. I was already bored with the beginner workshops so I figured I wanted to be challenged and I really wanted to push myself. I decided I would rather be the worst medium in an Advanced or Master class rather than one of the best in a beginner class. So then it was just a matter of packing my bags and heading off.

What courses did you end up taking at Arthur Findlay College?

The first week I took a course with Sandy Baker on Evidential Mediumship, then a platform mediumship course with Simon Key, followed by a course on Spirit Art with Lynn Cottrell. All of these tutors were excellent and I really enjoyed being surrounded by advanced and professional mediums. What surprised me the most was that I fit right in with them. I did not feel out of place at all and I was really happy with the readings I was able to give. I really appreciated the instruction and encouragement I was given because it really set me up for my second week where I took a session on advanced mediumship with Val Williams, Simon Key, Lynn Cottrell and Lynn Parker.

WHAT IS SPIRIT ART?

Spirit Art is one of the most amazing things that I experienced at Arthur Findlay College. On the first evening we were there, Simon Key and Lynn Cottrell gave a demonstration of Spirit Art during a spiritualist church service. Both mediums were on the platform at the front of the service. They connected with spirit and after making sure that they both had the same spirit they then turned to the audience. Simone started to give a traditional mediumship message. She started with incredible pieces of evidence and eventually narrowed it down to the one person in the audience for whom the reading was for. While she was doing this Lynn was drawing on an artist's easel beside her facing sideways to the audience so we could not see what see was drawing. Simon continued by giving the message and when she was finished Lynn revealed the drawing of the spirit who had come through. It was totally unbelievable and the person receiving the message was moved to tears. This was probably one of most powerful "wow" moments I have ever been a part of. There was a family visiting Arthur Findlay College that night who were scouting out the chapel because their son was getting married there on the weekend. The reading turned out to be for the groom and it was his grandfather. It was a beautiful message filled with love and well wishes. But to be able to take away a beautiful drawing of his grandfather only made the event more special. I was really hoping that my mother would come through for me during their second reading but alas it was not meant to be. On the third reading, Lynn closed her eyes and drew with two pieces of charcoal, one in each hand. It was amazing to watch and it reminded me of automatic writing. It was easy to see spirit working through her and creating the most amazing drawing of the spirit that was coming through.

WHAT DID YOU LEARNED AT ARTHUR FINDLAY COLLEGE?

During the day we had many different workshops where we learned a lot of specific techniques but what I really keyed in on was watching the tutors teach. I was fascinated by watching them work with the different students. A lot of people "zoned out" during the sessions where we all got turns to demonstrate our mediumship or to try new things. When there are 25 people taking turns doing readings, after the first few it can become a little tedious if you are not involved in the reading. However, I decided I would imagine I was the tutor and I would watch each of my colleagues as they took turns doing readings and tried to think of what I would say to them if I had to give them specific feedback. I imagined what I would say to them to help them become the best they could be. Then I would listen to what Val had to say to them to see if she saw the same things I did and if her feedback was the same or different. In the evenings, I would write out notes on what I had learned and then recorded them into affirmations. By doing this I was hoping that years later I could listen to them again and remember what I had learned. You can listen to this affirmation at https://www.alfromcanada.com/affirmations-by-albert-olson.html

I also asked a lot of questions of my fellow students about how they did things and what worked for them. For example at dinner I would ask, "What was the most amazing thing you learned today?" Or "What was the one thing that really helped you become a professional medium?" I guess I am a life long learner and teacher. I do believe this approach has really helped me in my role as a mediumship mentor and the work I do in the free online mediumship development circles that I host today.

WHAT AMAZING EXPERIENCES DID YOU HAVE AT AFC?

I experienced a lot of amazing things and people including: Physical Mediumship, a Trance Tent, Table Tipping, Psychometry, Trance Healing and synchronistic friendships.

WHAT IS PHYSICAL MEDIUMSHIP?

Mental mediumship is another name for what most people just call mediumship. It is when a medium receives a message from spirit through their various senses or "clairs". Usually they are the only person to receive these messages. Physical mediumship is when spirit actually communicates by giving messages through actual physical means and everyone present experiences the message. For example when you and everyone actually hears someone knocking on a door or when a spirit appears in physical form such as a ghost. Sometimes it includes the physical manifestation or manipulation of an object. At Arthur Findlay College one of the most interesting forms of physical mediumship that I experienced was "table tipping".

What is "Table Tipping"?

One night at Arthur Findlay College we attended a demonstration of "Table Tipping". We all gathered in a circle sitting in chairs. In the middle the workshop leaders brought a small three legged coffee table. They lightly put their hands on the edge of the table. It reminded me of how people lightly put fingers on an Ouija Board. The idea was that spirit was to work through the two mediums and be able to move the table around the room by rocking back and forth. I was really surprised when the table began to quickly rock back and forth, sometimes having only one leg remain in contact with the floor. Eventually the table would rock its way until it was right in front of someone sitting in the circle and sometimes it tipped or leaned right into the person's lap. At that point the mediums would give a message to the person sitting in the chair from the spirit that moved the table. Then it was like musical chairs and the person who received the message took the place of one of the leaders and they started in the middle of the circle again with a new spirit. At first I was very sceptical and felt for sure that the leaders must be moving the table by themselves and so when it was my turn I very consciously made sure that I was not manipulating the table in any way. I was quite surprised when the table started moving on its own. Eventually it moved and stopped right in the lap of my very good friend Angela whom I was able to give a message to. I was not surprised that the table was drawn to Angela because although we never met before that week, Angela and I were always somehow linked or drawn to each other in almost all the exercises and activities that we did that week. It was a prime example of a very strong spiritual connection. There was something very synchronistic about how we always got randomly paired up. In hindsight, I think we must have been connected spiritually in a past life. Other examples of physical mediumship included psychometry.

WHAT IS PSYCHOMETRY?

Psychometry is when a medium is able to give a reading based on the energy of an object. For example, a person brings a personal object of the spirit they want a reading for. It could be a watch or a piece of jewelry. The idea behind this activity is that an object that has been close to the spirit can absorb some of the spirit's energy. A good medium can sense the spirit's energy and this helps them to build a strong connection with them. Psychometry is often used in missing persons cases. Objects of the missing person are brought to a psychic or medium to help them make a connection with the missing person's energy in order for them to help locate the missing person. Other types of physical mediumship includes transmutation or transfiguration and the use of a "trance tent".

WHAT IS A "TRANCE TENT"?

During my visit to Arthur Findlay College I was able to experience a "trance tent". A "trance tent" is a tool used in physical mediumship. In years past a "trance tent" used to be called a "trance cabinet". The idea behind this equipment is that a medium will meditate in the same place at the same time every day. By doing this the power of the spirit's and the medium's energy will increase over time by usage in the same place. In older times the medium would sit in a wooden closet or cabinet but any closed in space would work. This is why some times it is called a "trance cabinet". The medium should be surrounded on three sides by walls with an opening in front of them. Sometimes the room is darkened and a red light is shone on the face of the medium. This makes it easier for the audience or other mediums to see changes in the medium's face. This is called transfiguration or transmutation. When I was Arthur Findlay College they used a portable changing tent as the cabinet thus it was called a "trance tent." A medium from our group would volunteer to go into the tent and to close their eyes and to meditate in order to sit with spirit. "Sitting in the Power" or "Sitting in Spirit" is mentioned in an earlier section of this book. The medium would choose another medium that they trusted to be their support medium. The support medium would sit right in front of the tent facing the medium sitting in spirit. Their job was to support the medium sitting in spirit by providing additional vibrational energy and to watch for any abnormal reactions. The rest of us became observers and were supposed to watch the medium's face for any changes in shape. At first I did not notice anything unusual but eventually Val suggested that I begin to blink my eyes. When I did what she suggested, a most amazing thing happened, every time I opened my eyes after blinking I began to see a different face in place of the medium's face. I realized that each new face represented a spirit that the medium in trance knew or was connected with. It was truly incredible. When my friend Patrick was in trance and I blinked my eyes I saw the face of a man who was missing the top of his head. It was severed off like the top of a soft boiled egg in an egg cup. I blinked my eyes again and the face was gone and was replaced by an old man with a long white beard. Later that night I met up with Patrick in the pub and I said to him, "That was amazing trance mediumship you did today." He asked me what I meant and so I told him about the man with the top of his head cut off. Patrick jumped up and yelled, "I know who that is!" It turned out that Patrick used to work with a man who repaired hydro lines and one day at work he fell from one of the hydro towers. His hit his head during the fall and took off the top of his head. Later on that same spirit came through during a different mediumship session and gave Patrick an amazing reading. Patrick told me later that he had been encouraged to attend Arthur Findlay College because he was having strange dreams and he did not know what to make of them. Patrick had come to Arthur Findlay College reluctantly and not totally convinced he believed in spirit communication. He told me that this piece of evidence from his friend was what convinced him that it could happen.

WERE THERE ANY DOWNSIDES TO ATTENDING ARTHUR FINDLAY COLLEGE?

Although attending Arthur Findlay College was a life changing event for me there were a few downsides. First of all travelling from British Columbia to London is very expensive. As well, although I was exposed to excellent mentorship and to a multitude of experiences, the doctrine that the college follows is very old and reluctant to change. They have several "rules" that you have to follow and that at times can be very limiting. For example, they would not allow anyone to predict future events in any of your readings. At first I thought that they did not believe it was something a person could do but later I found out that Britain has a law against making predictions which they call fortune telling. So the tutors from Arthur Findlay College were simply following the law, but the way they enforced this law made it seem like they were telling you it was something you were not capable of doing. They also taught that you could only connect with whatever spirit come through and that you cannot contact specific spirits individually. I know this is not true at least for me, because I have always been able to contact with whoever I wanted to. However, if you did not know better you might believe that it just was not possible. They also seem to stress that it takes a long time and a lot of training to become a medium or a minister.

WHAT ELSE WERE YOU EXPOSED TO ON YOUR JOURNEY?

Unfortunately on my journey there have been many political battles. I think that very early on you will have to decide if you want to be territorial or inclusive when dealing with other mediums. What I mean is that as you become more advanced and you start to do public readings, it is inevitable that you will come in contact with other psychics, mediums and spiritualist ministers. Many of them will be professional mediums who do mediumship as their main source of income and as a result, they can be quite territorial. For example, as I returned from Arthur Findlay College I was so excited that I had done so well. I could hardly wait to tell my local Spiritualist minister and circle leader, all about my experience. I made a powerpoint to share with her and I sent her an email asking if we could meet. Unfortunately, in my enthusiasm I said in my email that I thought I was ready to do mediumship during one of their church services. Well, as it turns out she is very territorial and was angered by my arrogance. So when I showed up to share my experience she focussed on telling me how much I still needed to learn and that despite what I had experienced that I was not an advanced medium and that I was just a raw beginner. She came from the old school where you had to spend twenty-five years in training before you could do mediumship. I was heart broken and nearly gave up mediumship right then. I realized that she was not going to be the supportive mentor I was looking for. A few years later, I made the fatal mistake of asking if she would consider allowing me to become a student minister in her church. Well, apparently I committed another unspoken rule of her church that you never ask to become a student minister, you have to wait to be asked. Apparently I still have another twenty three years of training to do. In my case this is very problematic because in another 23 years I will be 86 years old and will probably be attending services while on the other side.

Another sad thing that happened to me caused a split with a very good friend of mine at the time. A year after studying at Arthur Findlay College and another year of mediumship development I thought I would put my years of teaching experience to work and do an advanced mediumship course for a store in nearby Victoria. I had arranged it with the owner and set dates for it. However, unbeknownst to me, my friend also did courses and workshops for the same store. The owner told her that I was offering a new course and she said, "Oh, don't offer that course, Al is not qualified or advanced enough to teach it." The owner called me the next day and cancelled the course and refunded all the money. I was so hurt by my friend's actions. At that time she had just become a full time professional medium and somehow either consciously or unconsciously I think she became threatened by my new course. I think she thought she might lose some of her clients. Unfortunately, one of her best friends was another of my circle leaders and mentors. This mentor took my friend's side, kicked me out of her circle and still does not talk to me to this day. Anyway these are examples of some of the "unfortunate incidents" I have encountered. I now like to think that they were great learning experiences because as a result of that conflict, I decided that going forward, I would be inclusive as possible to fellow mediums and use my skills to help people. It is hard enough being accepted in this world as a medium and spiritualist without fighting with other mediums. A year ago, I was inspired by two of Spiritualism's principles that encourage people to take personal responsibility and to make amends, I reached out to my friend and to my former mentors and apologized for my actions and the misunderstandings that had happened. Unfortunately my former friend and mentor were unwilling to accept my apologies for what had happened and are still unfriendly. Maybe one day they will be able to forgive and forget.

The aforementioned experiences were very important in my development. I learned that it is very hard to become a professional medium in your hometown. People already know you from before and find it hard to believe that such a change can happen. Some mediums never do readings for friends and family because they know how hard it is to become an expert in your own inner circle. The most important thing I learned was that at some point in your journey you will have to develop your own personal philosophy. You have to decide what your motivation is for doing mediumship. I will talk more about this in the next section.

Mastering Mediumship

Book 3 - Advanced

Albert Olson

WHEN DID YOU BECOME AN ADVANCED MEDIUM?

After three years of my development I began to move from an intermediate to advanced medium. For me the difference is that as an advanced medium I had the confidence and knowledge to start helping and teaching others on their journey. So far the three stages of development for me have been: beginner, intermediate and advanced. As a beginner I was totally discovering my gifts and was very much in an information gathering stage. As an intermediate I went public with my gifts and began to do free readings for friends and family. Finally, as an advanced medium I began to do larger public demonstrations and to run my own online circles. In order to make this transition to become what I consider advanced, I had to develop a philosophical foundation. Although in the previous chapter I told of situations where I ran into conflict with other mediums and with my local spiritualist church I do believe those things happened for a reason. I believe that it is not what happens to you, but how you react to it that makes a situation good or bad. In other words I had to change my perception. When I first started mediumship and until I returned from Arthur Findlay College, I have to admit that I was really arrogant about my skills. I thought I had these special gifts and that I would one day become rich and famous because to them. I had visions of becoming the next "Long Island Medium" or Tony Stockwell or James Van Prague. I must have been very annoying to have as participant in a development circle. It is hard to teach someone who is always keen to go first and wanting to be treated as an equal right from the start. For this I apologize to my first mentors. I really appreciate how they helped me with my development and I learned many things from them. In hindsight I was trying too hard, too fast to show them how good I was. I was completely driven by ego. Struggling with ego is something that all mediums must deal with at some time in their development. If you truly believe that you are an instrument of spirit and that you are here simply to help spirits connect with living people, then really whether or not your reading was good or bad has very little to do with you. Just as all people are different so are all spirits. Some are advanced and experienced with mediumship, others are new souls and may never have done mediumship before. As well, spirits have different personalities just as they did on earth. One spirit may be outgoing and another introverted. Some share similar experiences and so are able to send messages that are more easily understood by you. I often remind people that sometimes readings do not go well, or they have trouble connecting, that if a reading goes wrong it may be that the medium has done nothing wrong but rather they just were not able to make the connection for some reason. If it is true that poor readings are not necessarily the medium's fault then it is equally true that great readings may have more to do with the spirit than the medium. My ego would like to take credit for the great readings and to dismiss the poor readings as spirit's fault. Unfortunately it does not work that way. My mediumship skills took a quantum leap forward when my motivation changed from becoming rich and famous to helping others. A person could spend thousands of dollars looking for the "magic bullet" that will turn them into an incredible medium. I must have spent over five thousand dollars in books, workshops and courses in my first three years alone. I know of other mediums who have spent much more than this. Many professional mediums are excellent mediums, but not many are trained teachers. As a retired teacher I was generally disappointed with the poor quality of instruction at the workshops I attended. The first workshop that I attended was quite exciting because it was all new. I was really thrilled, I had been able to give a couple of readings and to get some feedback. I had met several like-minded people and I went home happy. The following week the same person was offering another workshop. So I thought great and signed up. I was really disappointed that although the topic was published as being something different it was in fact the same workshop. I was not happy after the second workshop because of the lack of specific feedback. In my experience it did not seem to matter if you signed up for a beginners or an advanced course. The content seemed very similar and very general in nature. Due to the lack of personalized instruction, I often felt that I kept getting beginner instruction all the time. I was not getting my individual needs met. It was not until I got to Arthur Findlay College that I finally felt my needs were met. The tutors there really did give specific feedback and they did push me to expand my abilities. This was when I decided to develop a personal philosophy that centred on helping both people here in this world and those in spirit. As a result I created what I call my "Golden Rules".

What are your Golden Rules of mediumship?

GOLDEN RULES OF MEDIUMSHIP

- There is only one right way to do Mediumship and that is the way that is best for you. I can choose to be a second rate Long Island Medium or I can be the very best Al Olson that I can be. What works for one person may or may not work for another.
- We all have gifts, part of our journey is to figure out what they are and how we can best use them to help people.
- No negative self talk.
- Do not set limits on yourself. Do not let others tell you what you can and cannot do. You never know what spirit has in store for you.
- Treat others as you would like to be treated.
- Do not let ego be your motivation. Be motivated by a desire to help others rather than becoming rich and famous.
- Anyone can become a medium.

- Once you become open to receive messages, then any thought, image, sound or feeling that you experience comes directly from spirit.

- Spirit does not give you evidence for no reason. Everything they give you means something.

- Try everything to find out what works best for you.

- Do not be afraid of failure, often this is the best way to learn.

- Practice, practice, practice!

- When in doubt let Spirit guide you and lead you.

WHAT IS THE NEXT STEP TO BECOMING AN ADVANCED MEDIUM?

After defining your philosophical foundation the next thing to do is to find the right mentor who will understand you and allow you to progress on your spiritual journey. I was very lucky to find my true mentor. A wonderful man who was also a minister at our local spiritualist church. He also conducted a mediumship development circle. After some hesitation I approached Malcolm Gloster. He welcomed me to his circle and the rest has been history. I knew some of the people in his circle from before and I liked them. Malcolm has a unique way of allowing all his circle members to develop in their own way. He does not try to fit people into a mould of his creation or any other mould for that matter. He is an incredible medium in his own right but he is also an excellent mentor. I fit right in with his circle so much that we have become almost family. Twice a year we have retreats at a nearby sea side resort where one of our members owns a house. These are very special weekends where, with our significant others we gather for three days of laughs and experimenting with all things intuitive. We also do a free reading night for the local residents. We eat great food and spend a lot of time singing and laughing. It is so important to have a support system such as this so that you can have an opportunity vent and share and learn from like-minded people. I would encourage you to find such a mentor and support group because it is so important to be able to reach out to someone who understands your situation whenever you fall into one of the inevitable down periods that we all encounter from time to time. I realize how important it is to find the right mentor that is right for you. Many people do not have this possibility and so face the struggles of their journey alone.

WHERE CAN YOU FIND A MENTOR OR A DEVELOPMENT CIRCLE?

The next best thing to meeting face to face is to meet with a mentor or a circle online. My sister was in this situation, she lived 500 miles away from me in a town with no circles and no spiritualist church. That is why four years ago I decided that I would start a free weekly online development circle. It has developed and grown now over the years to become quite a successful circle. In the past calendar year we have had over 500 different mediums come to our circle from over 25 different countries of the world. It is truly awesome to have a place where mediums of all levels, from all over the world can come together to give readings, get readings and to share best practices. Some drop in and out, some come once and never come back and many have become full time regulars. You are most welcome to join. This is a free service. If you are interested please go to: www.alfromcananda.com/zoom to check out your options and to register.

www.alfromcanada.com/mediumship

WHAT ARE THE ADVANTAGES OF HOSTING YOUR OWN CIRCLES?

I learned many things about hosting my own online circle using the program called Zoom. What an amazing tool, I only wish it had been available while I was still teaching. It was also reinforced to me that the best way to learn something is to teach it. I have learned so much from talking and working with such a wide range of amazing mediums from all over the world. But the most amazing thing happened over the course of the past few years is that I learned how fast the world is changing, especially in the world of mediumship and spiritualism.

How is the world changing for mediums and spiritualists?

The world, because of social media, is becoming much smaller. My first mentor told me that it would take 25 years to become a medium and while at Arthur Findlay College this was reinforced in some of the writings in their library. In my view, that may have been true at one time, perhaps twenty years ago or longer. Back then you might have been lucky to have a spiritualist church that you could go to near by or a local development circle to attend but even then you would only go for one hour a week and it would be hit or miss whether your mentor or minister would be able to help you on your individual journey. In my case, before Zoom and online social media instruction, it probably would have taken fifty years to become a medium. However, in today's world you do not need to travel the world for instruction or to pay thousands of dollars for workshops because of the internet. You can practice every day all day long if you want. You can join as many groups or courses or workshops or circles as you can handle. You can give readings as a professional and never leave your home without anyone in your family knowing. I also believe that church services will also have to change and become live streamed or recorded to enlarge their congregation. There are many people out there who have never had the opportunity to attend a Spiritualist Church Service. This is why I have started an Online Spiritualist Church. For more information about this see the next section on becoming a Professional Medium. So it occurred to me that there is currently a revolution happening within the Medium / Spiritualist community. A revolution between old school mediumship and modern mediumship.

WHAT IS MODERN MEDIUMSHIP?

Classical or "Old School" mediumship is what has been traditionally taught since the late nineteenth century. It is how mediumship has been done until recently. It is conservative, slow and reluctant to change. Many traditionalists believe that mediumship is well-defined and that it takes decades to learn. There is one way, their way. This steadfast tradition will lead to the end of traditional spiritualist churches over the next forty years. The advent of the internet and social media has changed everything. Now a person can be exposed to a variety of mentors and spiritual leaders from all over the world at any time of day or night. People who want readings will have an endless choice of mediums to choose from. Mediums that do not adapt to these new ways will have a hard time continuing to build their practice with this new type of clientele. The internet revolution is also affecting the way that mediumship is done. It used to be you had to go and see a medium locally or call them on the phone to get a reading. Unless they knew you, there was no way for them to do background checks and so information such as a person's name, the make up of their family and what they liked to do. Until now these were all acceptable evidence for a medium to give. But now a person can quickly google someone's name or check them out on social media and in less than 5 minutes find out more information about them than ever before. This makes it very easy to act as a fraudulent medium but it also has meant that modern day mediums must now come up with more and different types of evidence than ever before. In order to do this they must try many new ways of getting evidence and push their comfort levels to try new things. Otherwise It will become harder and harder to convince a skeptic that you actually have one of their loved ones in spirit that is communicating with them. The classical tradition of striving for five pieces of evidence in less than five minutes just does not cut it any more. Modern day mediums must really make an emotional connection with spirit in order to provide sufficient evidence to give a meaningful message. "I have a woman who likes to bake that seems like your grandma and who is proud of you and loves you." just is not good enough any more. An advanced medium needs to be able to share evidence that will emotionally connect the client with the spirit beyond a doubt and to them give a meaningful message that will provide healing either for someone on this side or for spirits on the other or for both.

How do you give emotional relevant evidence in Modern Mediumship?

In order to give emotional relevant evidence in Modern Mediumship you must be able to tap into the emotions of the spirit through clairsentient messages. I have seen many mediums that can give an hour of evidence and then say for the message they just want to say hello and they love you and wrap it up in less than thirty seconds. Usually this often happens with beginners who are so excited they are getting any evidence at all that they keep going with the evidence and then have nothing for the message. This is usually because the medium is relying on clairvoyance primarily as their means of communication. At some point to give a meaningful message that promotes healing you have to tap into the emotions of the spirit. It is very difficult if not impossible to say why the spirit came through, what they wanted to say if you cannot tell what they are feeling. The best mediums that give the best messages, that provide the most healing are always excellent at receiving clairsentient messages. They can blend their energies with the spirit, they are sensitives and great empaths who can sense how the spirit is feeling and then can use those emotions to give a heart felt message. So advanced mediums are usually very good at receiving messages in a variety of ways but are also incredible at using their empathic skills to tap into the spirit's emotions to give a meaningful and healing message.

What else is new in Modern Mediumship?

There are amazing new ways of giving readings such as : paired readings, group readings, mixing psychic and mediumistic readings, using art, music, automatic writing and inspired singing in readings. As well modern mediumship tends to use a lot of symbolism in readings. I will briefly describe each of these new characteristics below.

WHAT ARE PAIRED READINGS?

As discussed earlier paired readings are becoming more common. This is where two mediums work together to give one reading. Brian Robertson and Simon James from the Open Door Spiritualist Church in Victoria British Columbia are the best I have ever seen as doing this. In fact it is the only way I have seen these two Arthur Findlay College tutors give readings. They demonstrate their paired mediumship weekly in their church services. This is also an excellent way for beginners to start giving public demonstrations as the "tag team" approach allows them the opportunity to regroup and to build their connection with spirit while the other person gives evidence. It also reduces stress because you are not on stage all alone.

What do you mean by group readings?

Group readings is similar to paired readings except that you have more than two mediums giving a reading. This is often a common characteristic of the type of practice that is demonstrated in a mediumship development circle. Usually one medium takes the lead but will ask for help from other mediums during the reading to see if they have anything to offer. The beauty of this type of reading is that the combined connection to spirit can really lead to powerful readings. It is also an excellent way to help beginning mediums gain experience.

CAN YOU MIX PSYCHIC AND MEDIUMSHIP READINGS?

There seems to be a real movement to throw off long time mediumship traditions and to try new ways of connecting with spirit without any limitations being set on how you make the connection. One common practice that is gaining in popularity is a combination of psychic readings and mediumistic readings. Commonly this is a reading that begins psychically with or without cards where the medium or psychic gives a reading to a live person. I find that it is nearly impossible for me to give a psychic reading currently without someone on the spirit side coming through to add to the reading. I was surprised though, how helpful using tarot or oracle decks can be while giving a mediumship session can be. I now use my cards in a variety of ways during my mediumship readings. The first time I was exposed to this practice was by my good friend Aylieh who had people draw a card from the deck called "Talking to Heaven" by James Von Prague once she had finished her mediumship reading for them. I was amazed how much this meant to people and how well it reinforced the messages that Aylieh had already given. I have since also started to use tarot and oracle cards regularly during my mediumship sessions. It all started one evening when our circle was doing readings for friends and family. This particular evening I was having a really hard time connecting with spirit. Finally after trying very hard to connect for over half an hour a voice finally Sid to me, "Go and get your cards!", so I jumped up and went and got one of my decks. I started shuffling the cards and suddenly the cards seemed to be jumping right out into my hands. When I looked at them something in the card jumped out or spoke to me and so I began to use this information as the basis for the evidence I was giving in my reading. For example, on one card the image of an apple caught my attention. I immediately knew that the apple represented education of some sort. I saw the the old image of bringing an apple as a gift for your teacher. This is what made me make the connection to education. In this case it meant teacher and I was able to give the piece of evidence that the spirit who was coming through had been a teacher. This turned out to be the piece of evidence that allowed me to connect that particular spirit to the right person to receive a message. Sometimes I will draw up to three cards during the evidence phase and more cards from different decks to help with the message. I allow intuition to help me choose which decks to use. I now believe that once I set my intention to open up to spirit, in other words,

to turn on my "Open for Business" sign, that anything that comes into my head is coming directly from spirit. So when I draw a card during a reading my attention is drawn to some aspect of the card by spirit to give me a hint or a guidepost to show me where to go with the reading.

For example I pull a card from John Holland's beautiful deck, The Psychic Tarot for the Heart Oracle Deck, my attention may be drawn to colour of the card or to the number at the top or to the words at the bottom or perhaps something in the picture will jump out at me. This gives me an idea where to go next with my evidence. Sometimes I will only use cards during the message section in conjunction with psychically reading the client to make the message they receive that more powerful. Please go to https://www.alfromcanada.com/tarot-and-oracle-deck-reviews.html to see the different decks I use.

WHAT IS SPIRIT ART?

A lthough, spirit art has been a long time tradition in Spiritualism, today we are seeing spirit art expanding to include such things as pottery, stain glass, knitting and photography. For a more detailed description of spirit art please refer to the section in part two of this book.

HOW DO YOU USE MUSIC TO GET MESSAGES FROM SPIRIT?

Music had also become a new area in which mediums are exploring a variety of new ways to use music in the readings. I regularly use my Google Home in conjunction with Spotify to help me use music in my readings. I am not a singer, in fact I have a really hard time even singing in key. Sometimes while giving a reading, I would be given the name of a song or some lyrics from a song. Sometimes I would mention this evidence to the the person getting the reading but often I was too embarrassed by my lack of singing skills to share this evidence. I often thought that the song or its lyrics could be incredibly powerful evidence. Imagine if spirit was able to share a loved one's favourite song with them, how powerful that would be. Then it occurred to me that with Google Home and Spotify I could access any song ever written and play it. This is an incredible tool because you can say to google, "Hey google, play the song about speaking words of wisdom" and it will reply, "Playing Let it Be by the Beatles. I will often listen to the song as it is being played and wait for a certain line to jump out at me, to speak to me. I will then use that line to help clarify the evidence or message being given. In our online circle we have been experimenting with playing a random song from Spotify and then using the feeling it

185

produces, the emotions associated with the song and the lyrics to begin a reading and to start the initial connection with spirit. Try it sometime or come and join us in our circle, it is a lot of fun.

WHAT IS "AUTOMATIC WRITING"?

Another new development is using automatic writing while giving a mediumship reading. By writing down the evidence and messages that you receive during a reading often helps a medium to get additional or more specific information. Automatic writing is described more fully in part two of this book and is usually done as a stand alone activity. What I am suggesting here is that you try automatic writing while giving a reading as the same time. I was surprised how much more information I could get during a reading if I began to write down the evidence and messages I was receiving. Try it and see if it works for you.

WHAT IS "INSPIRED SINGING"?

L ike Inspired speaking and automatic writing the medium allows spirit to inspire the lyrics and music without any preparation. This is a very powerful demonstration of a different type of mediumship. I like to think that inspired singing is the spiritualist's way of singing rap music.

How do use symbolism in your readings?

Finally the use of symbolism in readings has become more and more common. I now find that if I give evidence and the sitter says, "No I can't take that" it is often an indication that the message or evidence is not a literal message but rather something symbolic that has either significance to me or the sitter. Remember that spirit does not give you information for no reason. The information must mean something, it is just a matter of figuring out the connection. If your normal way of receiving information is not making sense to the sitter then try using symbolism instead. As I mentioned earlier in this book, I once was giving a reading and the image of an apple came to me. After giving clues like, "I see and apple, this person was a farmer" and receiving a series of no's, I began to think that the apple was symbolic evidence rather than literal and so I began to make the connection to education. Now whenever I see an apple during a reading, I immediately realize that the spirit that is coming through, is connected to education in some way. Try using symbolism and begin to build your own dictionary of symbols to use with spirit.

WHAT ARE SOME OF THE CHALLENGES OF BEING AN ADVANCED MEDIUM?

There are many challenges to being an advanced mediums and they are not the same for every person. For example as you become more advanced you have to learn how to handle more than one spirit at a time and you also become more adept at working with issues such as the ethical way to handle delicate situations such as suicides and the death of a child or family member. In certain situations, such as in a public demonstration or a church service, it is probably not advisable to bring up certain sensitive issues such as suicides or the death of a child. In these cases it is advisable to suggest that you meet with the sitter privately in order to complete the reading. So the issue becomes ethically, whether or not you should share all the information you are receiving with the sitter. Of course the answer is it depends. As you gain confidence and experience you become better at knowing when to say something and when not to depending on the time and situation. More importantly it is choosing the appropriate words or way to deliver a message. It is important to be tasteful and tactful. As in everything else let spirit guide you.

Mastering Mediumship

Book 4 - Professional

How do you become a
professional medium?

About a year ago, I made the transition from being an advanced medium to becoming a professional. For me becoming a professional has nothing to do with making money. Rather it is a change in the type of work that l am doing for spirit. It is a change in the amount of time I spend doing mediumship and the type of audience I am working with. It involves going from being a local expert to becoming a nationally or internationally recognized medium and mentor. There are many ways to raise your profile and the path taken can be different for each medium. For me it was never about making money but instead it has always been about helping and healing people. But for others it is a combination of helping people and through an exchange of energy, or an exchange of services they are ok with accepting donations or fees for their services. I understand and support this completely. Others feel that it is only normal to be paid for their time and effort. I understand and support this as well. They would argue that doctors are well compensated for their training and expertise so therefore there is nothing wrong in accepting a fair wage for their time and services. I understand and completely support all three of these positions. Just as each medium receives messages differently, I feel that in terms of compensation this too will depend on the medium, the circumstances and their motivation for doing their work. There are many mediums who at this point begin to think about quitting their day jobs and to becoming a paid full time professional medium as their main source of income. I believe that it is nearly impossible to this without a large international following. Once you become well-known and develop a large following, it allows you to charge more for your individual readings but also allows you to supplement this income with other income sources or income streams.

WHAT ARE SOME OTHER INCOME STREAMS THAT PROFESSIONALS CAN PURSUE?

There are many ways to develop numerous income streams. These include but are not limited to:

1. Personal Readings both online and in person.
2. Running Circles both online and in person.
3. Providing training through a variety of workshops and courses.
4. Writing books and articles.
5. Creating Oracle and Tarot Decks.
6. Providing short term and long term mentorship.
7. Running a podcast or online radio station.
8. Creating or being an administrator for social media groups.
9. Creating, running and or participating in a spiritualist church.
10. Creating meditations and affirmations recordings for sale.
11. Becoming an influencer on social media.
12. Creating a YouTube Channel.
13. Creating a popular website where you can sell advertising.
14. Doing a weekly local radio show.
15. Doing a television show.

16. Providing technical support for other presenters using Zoom or other online communication software.
17. Working for large psychic companies who provide readings by telephone.
18. Creating an online zoom or face to face psychic reading service company similar to the telephone one mentioned above.

For me so far the first ten have become a reality and has helped me improve and develop a global presence. It has also allowed me to help many more people. Really successful professional mediums usually have multiple sources of revenue. They will do private readings for several hundred dollars a reading but they will have also published a book or several books. They may have several tarot or oracle decks that they have created and marketed. In addition they may have Mp3 or CD recordings of meditations, visualizations or affirmations that are available for purchase. They may have a weekly or daily podcast or radio show that increases their exposure or allows for paid subscribers as well as the selling of advertising. A large part of their income will come from doing instruction through mentorship, courses, workshops and week-long retreats. These can be done both online and in person. They will also do demonstrations of mediumship either online or most likely in person. People will pay money to watch the medium work and do their demonstration of platform mediumship. However, at the same time there will be an opportunity for private or small group readings later as well the opportunity to sell copies of their books, decks and cd's available with other merchandise such as crystals, t-shirts, other books and decks that they can sell at a slight marked up price. In other words they have become much more than a person giving readings and instead have created their own brand.

WHAT DO YOU NEED TO CONSIDER WHEN BECOMING A PROFESSIONAL?

I think the same ethical considerations have to be decided upon as a professional as were made when you first began doing readings for people. What is your prime motivation for doing this work? Is it to make money, or to help people? Is it possible to do both without compromising your principles? Will you work full-time or part-time. It is virtually impossible to make a full time living by simply doing readings. In order to become a full time professional psychic /medium you have to generate multiple income streams that continue to produce income year after year. You have to become a "Jack Of All Trades", good at many things. You need to be willing to travel. You have to keep up with ever changing fads and popular culture. You need to be able to be flexible and to find new ways to deliver your message and to fulfill your destiny. You need to stay up to date with current fads and with the advancement in technology. For example, I came up with an excellent idea for an Oracle deck. Many times in readings I wanted my clients to be able to communicate with spirit directly themselves. I had had great success using cards in my mediumship readings, especially

James Van Praagh's deck called"Talking to Heaven" which was mentioned earlier in this book. I kept looking for a deck that would help people identify signs or symbols from spirit. It would be called, "Signs from Spirit," I started polling people in my circles and on social media about the different signs they had received from spirit. I came up with over a hundred different ways and then I narrowed it down to the seventy-two most common ones. Then for over four years I tried to find an illustrator who wanted to work with me. No luck, some were interested but did not have time, some just thought I was crazy. In the end spirit came to me one night in a meditation and told me to do it myself. I laughed out loud. Anyone who had seen me play Pictionary knew I was a stick man artist at best. So then, I had an idea, what if I used a picture instead of a drawing? So I went on line and found a website called Pexel.com, where photographers from all over the world share their beautiful pictures royalty free. Then I remembered an app on my phone called "Artisto" where you can take a photo, and apply different filters to it to make it look like a painting. Voila, after some searching and editing, I was able to create my deck. The next step would be to figure out how to produce it. I could submit it to various publishers to see if they were interested, and I might still do that at some point. But for now, I mostly wanted the deck for myself, my friends, family and circle members. I tried Staples and a few other printing stores but the cost was going to be between $50 and $100 a deck. Then I found a company that makes custom playing cards, MakePlayingCards.com and one of their options was custom tarot decks. I submitted my 72 cards plus six explanation cards to make a deck of 78 cards for about US$17 a deck. The beautiful thing about this company is that they will print the decks and ship them to your customers directly. This saves the customers time and money. If you are interested in purchasing a copy of this deck please check out my website at: www.alfromcanada.com/signs-from-spirit-oracle-cards where there is a special tab just for this deck.

WHAT DO YOU CONSIDER WHEN STARTING A BUSINESS?

There are so many things to consider when starting a business or creating a brand but for sure you will need to create a logo for your brand. I think it is worth having a professional graphic designer create one for you based on images that are related to your name or your beliefs. A cheaper way to get this done is to find a local university or college that offers graphic design courses and ask the professor if there is a student they would recommend to you to do your logo. Students often are looking for ideas for their projects and a little extra income on the side can come in quite handy for them. Once you have your logo then you can create business cards. I used Vistaprint.com for my business cards as well as some fridge magnets and a poster board for when I am working at a fair or demonstration. I found their rates to be the cheapest and their quality of work to be excellent. Creating a website is also very important. You will need to pay a yearly fee for your URL. A URL is your domain name. My URL is "www.alfromcanda.com" This is the name of your website address that you use for people to find you on the internet. I used the site Weebly.com to create my website. It was very user friendly and was much like using a word processor. Weebly also offers to sell you URL's and email addresses that you can assign to your web site. Then you will need some way to collect money. I use PayPal which can be incorporated into your website easily and most people are familiar with this type of payment. On your website you should dedicate one of its pages as a review page. When ever I receive a positive comment by email or on facebook, I copy the comments and paste them onto the review section of my website. Check mine out at www.alfromcanada.com/reviews. Finally once you have your website up and running you want people to be able to find it when they do a search for mediums or psychic readings etc. In order for your website address to come up on the first page of search results you will need to do what is called Search Engine Optimization or SEO for short. You can pay for this service by finding a company who will offer to do SEO for you and you have to decide if the increase traffic flow to your website from the SEO you paid for is worth it. In other words does the additional business it brings in provide more income that the cost of paying for the SEO. These are just a few of the things to consider as you become a professional. If you need help with any of the things I have mentioned above please feel free to contact me for help. I will even set up your on line services for a fee.

ANY LAST WORDS?

I just want to wish you the very best of luck on your spiritual journey. Remember to enjoy the moment and to focus on the process and not the destination. If I can be of any help to you please contact me at: al.olson0@me.com or visit my web page at www.alfromcanada.com

ABOUT THE AUTHOR

Al is a retired school teacher who has taught in both the private and public systems at all levels for over thirty years. He is also a registered clinical hypnotherapist and a sport psychology consultant with a Masters Degree in Coaching. He has refined his psychic and mediumistic skills by attending advanced and master classes at Arthur Findlay College, the world's foremost college for the advancement of spiritualism and psychic sciences. He has hosted free weekly online mediumship development circles since 2016. He is a world class medium and instructor of all things intuitive. He is also the founder and host of the Online Franciscan Spiritualist Church.

PRAISE FOR THE AUTHOR

Al Olson is an amazingly intuitive medium! He offers a grounded and open perspective through which Spirit speaks. He is clearly very well-educated and he brings a broad awareness of spiritual teachings to his readings. He also brings a very open, loving and compassionate heart to everyone he works with. I would highly recommend seeing Al for a reading, you will be delighted and comforted with the messages he brings through.

Sarah Wilson

Co-ordination Cowichan Healing Arts Expo

Wow wow wow! THANK YOU so much. I will do all of the steps you have laid out. You are quite a teacher. I hope people are supporting you well. You are a wonderful teacher and an incredibly gracious person. Thank you so much!

Debra

Thank you so much for the wonderful reading. It was most helpful. I have experienced many readings over my lifetime, but yours was different. As is so often the case, I receive helpful tools from a reading, and I did so with your reading, but I have never before received a healing. This was a surprise to me. After the reading, I felt the anger increase and then totally dissipate! I had been carrying it for 3 weeks as well as a very heavy weight of sadness upon my chest, which has now mostly gone. So it seems, Albert, that you are a healer and a reader at the same time!

Karen

I just wanted to say thank you again for inviting me into your group. I was so impressed by your guidance and willingness to talk from spirit without much visual or verbal feedback from us in the group. I felt a lot of people were concentrating really hard. Three things really imprinted on my mind in addition to your willingness to share and teach and entertain.

I enjoyed the discussion of symbols and processes used by people, the different approaches. I learned a lot. Your invocation and prayer I felt was really comprehensive without being laboured. I really liked it, opened to it, felt safe by it.

When we sat with spirit for any messages, I found your leading of us into it and verbal coaching was just so revelatory and "in the moment" exactly what I responded to in terms of receiving what I got, and what to look and listen for. And thank you for your coaching in terms of summing up the evidence received and presenting the messages to people in the group. Great teaching. I got a lot of learning tonight from this group. It also had a really warm atmosphere (due largely to your leadership); it was like we were sitting around in a living room together. So thank you again.

Megan

Thank you for the last session,

Can't express in words how grateful I am for being directed to you and your beautiful circle

As it is the right place for me now.

Doron

I believe that this is the day we should give thanks to the special people we have met in our lives. So on this day I choose to thank you for all the wonderful conversations we have had in the passed and the guidance you have given me. Thank you for always making time for me. Bless you

Barbara

Albert Olson thank you for your time, your love and your light for the world. and I am grateful for being part of this group that you are sourcing. Thank you for being generous.

Randy

Hi Albert,

I so appreciate you and your advice and teachings.

Blessings Dawn

I love you

Albert is a very good instructor in mediumship, full of warmth and passion. The session was so lively! I am very grateful that I could attend to the circle online. I was searching for that kind of session since quite a long time now. Thank you Albert, I send you a lot of sunshine from France !

Melanie

SIGNS FROM SPIRIT ORACLE DECK

This is an oracle deck that I created to help your clients receive signs or messages from loved ones in Spirit. A collection of 72 pictures of signs that spirits use to send messages to let us know that they love us. Have a person think of their loved one in spirit and then draw a card. Whatever picture is on the card is a symbol of something the person should look for in their life because they will very soon experience what Is on the card and when they do they will know their loved one in spirit is thinking of them and sending them a message of love and reassurance that everything will be alright.

To order your own deck please www.alfromcanada.com/signs-from-spirit-oracle-cards . It costs $19.98 US plus shipping.

Franciscan Spiritualist Church

Come and join us for our online Spiritualist Church Service based on Franciscan Principles.

Go to www.alfromcanada.com for more info.

FREE ONLINE MEDIUMSHIP DEVELOPMENT CIRCLE

I host a free online mediumship development circle where we study the best practices shared by mediums from all over the globe. All levels, from beginners to professionals, welcomed. Instruction and practice are divided according to level. Would you be interested in joining us?

Go to www.alfromcanada.com/mediumship.

Contact Information

Albert Olson

www.alfromcanada.com

alfromcanada@gmail.com